KEN[T]UCK[Y]

COOK BOOK

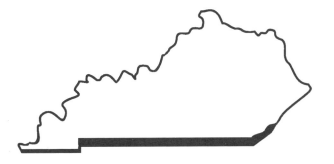

Cooking Across America
Cook Book Series™

**GOLDEN
WEST** ☼
PUBLISHERS

Front cover photo courtesy National Pork Producers Council
Back cover photo courtesy of the Kentucky Derby Museum, Gate
#1, Churchill Downs, Louisville, Kentucky

Photo (page 37) of Colonel Harland Sanders,
courtesy Kentucky Fried Chicken Corporation,
Louisville, KY

Acknowledgments

A special thanks to Tammy Lubash of Louisville
for recipe compilation and editing services.

Printed in the United States of America

ISBN #1-885590-64-4

Golden West Publishers, Inc.
4113 N. Longview Ave.
Phoenix, AZ 85014, USA
(602) 265-4392

Visit our website: www.goldenwestpublishers.com

Table of Contents

Table of Contents (continued)

Kentucky!

Introduction

Welcome to the Bluegrass State! Kentucky cuisine has had many influences: Native Americans, African Americans, early settlers, farmers, socialites and celebrity chefs. Kentucky is a state of varied regions, from Louisville to Central Kentucky and Appalachia, Kentucky cooking has represented the best of the South, country farms and cultural environs surrounding the Kentucky Derby. There are many ethnic influences reflected in Kentucky dining; this book presents a delicious sampling of many of the foods that are unique to Kentucky.

Kentucky is a state rich in history and resources. The *Kentucky Cook Book* includes traditional Derby recipes such as *The Derby Café's Mint Julep, Benedictine Sandwich* and *Kentucky Derby Pie,* as well as favorites like *Kentucky Hot Brown, Poke Sallet* and *Old-Fashioned 9-Layer Stack Cake.* You'll find a great *Burgoo* recipe, a *Henry Bain Sauce* and recipes for *Cabin Grits Fritters, Fried Green Tomatoes, Bourbon Brownies* and many more! The recipes in *Kentucky Cook Book* have been submitted by country cooks, celebrity chefs and well-known Kentuckians from throughout the state.

Take your time as you read through these pages–most of the recipes have a charming history, providing a glimpse of the many ethnic and cultural influences that helped shape Kentucky into the great state it is today. As part of Golden West's Cooking Across America Cook Book Series, *Kentucky Cook Book* will become a great keepsake and souvenir.

Kentucky Facts

Size – 37th largest state with an area of 40,395 square miles
Population – 3,960,825
State Capital – Frankfort, capital since 1792
Statehood – June 1, 1792; the 15th
　　state admitted to the Union
State Song – "My Old Kentucky Home"
　　by Stephen Foster
State Nickname – The Bluegrass State
State Motto – United we stand,
　　divided we fall
State Tree – Tulip Poplar
State Flower – Goldenrod
State Fish – Bass
State Gemstone – Pearl

The State Bird
Cardinal

The State Animal
Grey Squirrel

Famous Kentuckians

　　Abraham Lincoln, *16th U.S. President*; Diane Sawyer, *news anchor;* Muhammad Ali, *athlete;* Ned Beatty, *actor;* Loretta Lynn, *singer;* Robert Penn Warren, *author;* Henry Clay, *politician;* Tom T. Hall, *entertainer;* Lee Majors, *actor;* Kentucky Headhunters, *musical group;* The Judds, *entertainers;* Chuck Woolery, *game show host;* Dwight Yoakum, *singer,* PeeWee Reese, *athlete;* Johnny Depp, *actor;* Mary Lincoln Todd, *first lady;* Christopher "Kit" Carson, *frontiersman;* Daniel Boone, *frontiersman;* Darrel Waltrip, *race car driver.*

Useful Information

Visitors:
　　Travel Department 1-800-225-8747
Recreation:
　　Dept. of Parks 1-800-255-7275
Fishing & Hunting Regulations:
　　Dept. of Fish and Wildlife Resources 1-502-564-4336
National Forest Information: Daniel Boone National Forest
　　U.S. Forest Service 1-606-745-3100
　　Reservations 1-877-444-6777

Kentucky Party Poppers

"This is a great party pleaser and goes really fast! Be sure to make enough for everyone to enjoy."

Joane Cook—Florence

2 pkgs. (12 ct. ea.) PARTRIDGE® DINNER ROLLS
1 1/2 lbs. HAM, shaved
8 oz. SWISS CHEESE, shredded
1 1/2 sticks BUTTER
2 Tbsp. WORCESTERSHIRE SAUCE
3 Tbsp. POPPY SEEDS

Cover a baking sheet with aluminum foil, leaving enough to pull up into a "dome top" for baking. Slice dinner rolls in half. Set tops aside and place bottoms on baking sheet. Place ham on bottoms then sprinkle with cheese. In a small saucepan, melt butter; add Worcestershire sauce and poppy seeds and heat for 1 minute. Drizzle 1/2 of butter mixture over cheese and then place tops on rolls and drizzle with remaining butter mixture. Pull foil up to cover completely. Bake at 400° for 10 minutes. Serve warm. May be made ahead of time and refrigerated until ready to bake.

Kentucky Kernel Sausage Balls

Hodgson Mill, Inc.—Hopkinsville

2 cups KENTUCKY KERNEL® SEASONED FLOUR
2 lbs. MILD BULK SAUSAGE
2 cups shredded SHARP CHEDDAR CHEESE

Mix all ingredients together. Form into balls about 1-inch in diameter and place on an ungreased cookie sheet. Bake at 350° for about 20 minutes. Remove from cookie sheet and allow to drain on paper towels. Serve warm. Sausage balls may be frozen for several weeks. When needed, remove from freezer and heat in warm oven.

Makes 8-9 dozen sausage balls.

Louisville

Home of the Kentucky Derby, in which the world's best 3-year-olds race on the first Saturday in May. The Derby, held at Churchill Downs, is the oldest continuously held horse race in the country. Louisville is also known for producing more than half of the world's supply of bourbon.

Bourbon Doggies

Laura Lee Harpring—Louisville

1 lb. FRANKFURTERS
3/4 cup BOURBON
1/2 cup KETCHUP

1/4 cup packed BROWN SUGAR
2 Tbsp. minced ONION

Cut franks into 1/2-inch slices. Combine remaining ingredients in a bowl, add franks and marinate for 4 hours. Place mixture in a saucepan and simmer for 10 minutes then transfer to a chafing dish to serve.

Serves 12.

Sweet Potato Puffs

"These are easy to make and everyone loves them, especially at Thanksgiving. Sweet potatoes are plentiful in the fall here."

Martha N. Robertson—Brandenburg

1-2 lbs. SWEET POTATOES, peeled and chunked
1 bag (10 oz.) large MARSHMALLOWS
1 pkg. (7 oz.) COCONUT FLAKES

In a saucepan, place sweet potatoes and enough water to cover. Cook until potatoes are tender; drain and then mash until smooth. With hands, take enough cooled sweet potato to cover each marshmallow and shape into a ball. Gently roll the balls in coconut and place on a baking sheet. Refrigerate. When ready to serve, bake puffs in a 375° oven until marshmallows begin to melt (or place under broiler for a few minutes).

Kentucky Bluegrass

The term's origin is unclear; the plant is green, but in the spring it produces bluish purple buds, possibly the source of its name. Reports say that the pioneers found this plant growing wild when they first came to Kentucky.

Spicy Bits

"This is my original recipe and many of my friends have asked for it."

Mary Ann Jeffries—Henderson

1 lb. ALL-MEAT BULK SAUSAGE
1 ONION, finely chopped
1 GREEN BELL PEPPER, finely chopped
1 lg. jar (16 oz.) CHEESE WHIZ®
1 pkg. (8 oz.) OROWHEAT® PARTY RYE BREAD

In a large skillet, cook sausage, onion and bell pepper together; drain well. Add enough Cheese Whiz to thicken and hold ingredients together. Spread a teaspoonful of mixture on each slice of bread and place on a baking sheet. Bake at 350° until bread is toasted. Serve warm or at room temperature.

Barbecued Meatballs *

"This is my 'most asked for' recipe. It can be a great appetizer, or a tasty entree."

Lauren Russell—Verona

Meatballs:

3 lbs. GROUND BEEF
1 can (12 oz.) EVAPORATED MILK
5½ oz 1 cup OATMEAL
4 oz 1 cup CRACKER CRUMBS
2 EGGS
1/2 cup chopped ONION
1/2 tsp. GARLIC POWDER
2 tsp. SALT
1/2 tsp. PEPPER
1-2 tsp. CHILI POWDER

Sauce:

2 cups KETCHUP
4 oz 1 cup packed BROWN SUGAR
1/2 tsp. LIQUID SMOKE, or to taste
1/2 tsp. GARLIC POWDER
1/4 cup chopped ONION

In a large mixing bowl, combine all ingredients for meatballs; mix well. Shape into walnut-size balls. Place in a 9 x 13 baking pan. In a medium mixing bowl, combine all ingredients for sauce; stir until sugar is dissolved, then pour over meatballs. Bake at 350° for 1 hour. When cool, add a toothpick to each and serve either hot or cold.

Did You Know?

Cumberland Falls, near Corbin, is the largest waterfall in Kentucky while Yahoo Falls, near Whitney City, is Kentucky's highest waterfall.

Olive Nut Spread

Trudie D. Reed—Reed Valley Orchard, Paris

1 pkg. (8 oz.) CREAM CHEESE, softened
1/2 cup chopped GREEN OLIVES
1/2 cup chopped PECANS
1/4 cup SALAD DRESSING or MAYONNAISE

In a bowl, beat cream cheese until smooth. Fold in olives and pecans and stir in salad dressing. Serve with crackers or on dark bread triangles.

Shrimp Balls

Lynda Mays—Lexington

1 lb. uncooked SHRIMP, peeled and deveined
1 EGG
Dash of PEPPER
1 GREEN ONION, minced
1/4 lb. WATER CHESTNUTS, finely chopped
1/2 tsp. SALT
1/4 tsp. GINGER
1 tsp. DRY WHITE WINE

Mix all ingredients well. Roll into small balls and deep fry until golden. Serve with **Mustard Sauce** on the side.

Mustard Sauce

3/4 cup MAYONNAISE   1 Tbsp. LEMON JUICE
1 Tbsp. DIJON MUSTARD   3/4 cup HEAVY CREAM, whipped

Combine mayonnaise, mustard and lemon juice. Fold in whipped cream.

Rattlesnake Hill Farm's Garlic Salsa

Jim and Megan Alexander—Rattlesnake Hill Farm, Bloomfield

2 cloves GARLIC
1 ONION, chopped
1 TOMATO, chopped
1/2-1 JALAPEÑO PEPPER, minced
1 sm. bunch CILANTRO, chopped
1/2 cup LIME JUICE
TORTILLA CHIPS

In a serving bowl, combine all ingredients. Set bowl in the center of a platter and surround with tortilla chips.

Makes 1 cup.

Pickled Eggs

This recipe is from Mrs. Patton's great-grandmother.

Governor Paul and Mrs. Judy Patton—Frankfort

2 jars (16 oz. ea.) tiny whole PICKLED BEETS
1 pt. RED VINEGAR
Whole CLOVES
1 Tbsp. GARLIC SALT
1 Tbsp. SUGAR
24 med. EGGS

Drain juice of both jars of beets into a bowl. Add one of the jars of beets and the next four ingredients to the beet juice. (Save the second jar of beets for another use). Mix ingredients well, then pour into a wide-mouthed sterilized, clear jar. Place eggs in a saucepan, cover with water and cook until hard-boiled. While eggs are still hot, peel and add to the pickle mixture in jar. Let stand at room temperature for 3 hours, then refrigerate until ready to use.

Did You Know?
Mildred and Patricia Hill, two sisters from Louisville, wrote "Happy Birthday To You."

"Henry Bain" Sauce

"This sauce makes a great dip, when thinned with mayonnaise and sour cream. It can also be thinned with oil and vinegar and used on salads. This is a traditional sauce of Louisville and is used often on ham, steak and french fries."

Laura Lee Harpring—Louisville

1 btl. (10 oz.) WORCESTERSHIRE
   SAUCE
1 btl. (10 oz.) A-1® SAUCE
1 jar (18 oz.) CHUTNEY, chopped

1 btl. (12 oz.) CHILI SAUCE
1 btl. (20 oz.) KETCHUP
Dash of TABASCO®

Combine all ingredients, cover and refrigerate until ready to use.

Front Porch Sippin' Tea

"This is a fruited tea that we have served guests for years. It's great for that special 'Derby Day' party."

Mike Stone—Old Stone Inn, Simpsonville

3 cups WATER
4 cups SUGAR
6 cups PINEAPPLE JUICE
1 1/4 cups ORANGE JUICE

1 cup LEMON JUICE
1 gal. TEA
GINGER ALE
Fresh MINT LEAVES

In a large mixing bowl, combine water and sugar; stir until sugar dissolves and mixture forms a syrup. Add juices and tea; stir well. To serve, fill glasses with ice, add tea mixture and splash with ginger ale. Garnish with mint.

Wassail

Marie Cubine—Louisville

2 qts. unsweetened APPLE JUICE
5 cups unsweetened PINEAPPLE JUICE
2 cups ORANGE JUICE
1 cup LEMON JUICE
1 cup SUGAR
1 tsp. whole CLOVES
1 stick CINNAMON

In a 1-gallon container, mix all ingredients together; let stand overnight. Heat and serve.

Le-Tang-Tea

"This recipe is an original that I have made for thirty years."

Frances Nell Blanc—Brandenburg

1/2 cup TANG®
1/4 cup INSTANT TEA
1/4 cup LEMON JUICE

1 3/4 cups SUGAR
3 Tbsp. SWEETENER

In a 1-gallon container, mix all ingredients together. Stir as you fill container with water then refrigerate.

Martha Nell's Wassail

"I have used this recipe for years as a special drink for family and friends during the holidays."

Martha N. Robertson—Brandenburg

1/2-3/4 cup packed BROWN SUGAR
6 whole CLOVES
1/2 stick CINNAMON

3 1/2 cups CRANBERRY JUICE
4 1/2 cups APPLE JUICE

In the basket of an electric coffee pot, combine sugar, cloves and cinnamon. Pour juices into pot, then allow to perk through one cycle. Serve hot.

Dixie Sparkle

"My grandmother served this unique punch at Christmas, probably to impress the neighbors. She was known as an 'uppity southern lady!'"

Lynn Green—Waddy

3-4 BANANAS, mashed
1/4 cup frozen ORANGE JUICE
3 Tbsp. LEMON JUICE
1/2 cup SUGAR

1 cup WATER
GINGER ALE
VANILLA ICE CREAM

In a blender, mix together the first 5 ingredients; blend for a few seconds. Pour mixture into ice cube trays and freeze until firm. To serve, place 2 cubes in each punch cup, let stand for 15-20 minutes and then fill cups with ginger ale. Add a scoop of vanilla ice cream for an extra sparkle.

The Derby Cafe's Mint Julep

Clements Catering and The Derby Cafe—Louisville

2 sprigs fresh MINT
1/2 oz. SIMPLE SUGAR SYRUP
BOURBON

Muddle mint and syrup in bottom of a julep glass. Pack the glass with crushed ice and pour bourbon over top until full. Garnish with another fresh mint sprig. Serve with a straw.

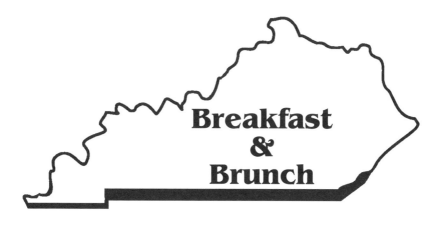

Breakfast & Brunch

Kentucky Derby Eggs

"This is a delicious breakfast casserole."

Carrie Fulkerson—Sonora

2 Tbsp. BUTTER
1/2 cup chopped ONION
2 Tbsp. ALL-PURPOSE FLOUR
1 1/4 cups MILK
1 cup shredded CHEESE
6 hard-boiled EGGS, sliced
1 1/2 cups crushed POTATO CHIPS
10 slices BACON

Preheat oven to 350°. In a small skillet, melt butter. Add onions and brown. Blend in flour, add milk and cook until mixture thickens. Add cheese and stir until melted. Layer half of the eggs, cheese sauce, potato chips and bacon in a baking dish then repeat layers. Bake at 350° for 30 minutes.

Poke Sallet
(Letcher County Style)

"I serve this as a breakfast, a salad or a side dish."

Kathryn Bale—Frankfort

Gather **1/2 gal. container** of young **POKEWEED** and wash well. Place pokeweed in a saucepan and parboil. Drain thoroughly. In a skillet, heat **1 cup PORK** or **CHICKEN DRIPPINGS.** Add poke to skillet and when it starts to bubble, add **1/2 cup CORNMEAL.** Stir. When cornmeal is done, stir in **2 or 3 scrambled EGGS.** Serve hot.

Serves 2.

Pokeweed, Pokeberry

Pokeweed is a stout, widely branched plant that grows 4-9 feet tall. It has red stems and oblong leaves (4-12 inches long). The flowers are followed by dark purple berries. The roots and seeds are poisonous, but the young shoots and leaves are edible and often included in Kentucky cuisine.

Pig-in-the-Poke Breakfast

"Our Poke Sallet Festival is celebrated on the first full weekend of June. People come from far and wide to savor the flavor of this very special Kentucky plant."

Gladys Haskins—Harlan County Chamber of Commerce, Harlan

4 slices COUNTRY HAM, fried
1 bunch POKE SALLET GREENS, boiled
2 hard-boiled EGGS

Place ham on a large platter, surround with well cooked and seasoned poke and garnish with sliced eggs. Best served hot.

Serves 4.

Peaches & Cream Cheese ✱ French Toast

"I have never before submitted any of my original recipes for a contest. This is one of many that my guests rave about!"

JoAnn Young Bland—Coffee Tree Cabin Bed & Breakfast,
Bardstown

1 can (15 oz.) sliced PEACHES*
1 1/2 cups packed LIGHT BROWN SUGAR
1/2 stick BUTTER or MARGARINE
6 slices BREAD
1 pkg. (8 oz.) CREAM CHEESE, softened
2 dashes CINNAMON
5 EGGS
3/4 cup MILK
1 1/2 Tbsp. VANILLA
1/2 cup BLACKBERRY or RASPBERRY SYRUP

Drain peaches, reserving syrup and set aside. Place sugar, butter and 1/4 cup peach syrup in a 9 x 13 baking dish and microwave until mixture thickens. Layer peaches over top of syrup mixture. Spread half of the cream cheese on one side of each slice of bread and lay the slices, cheese side down, on top of the syrup. Spread the balance of the cream cheese on top of the bread slices and then sprinkle with cinnamon. In a bowl, beat eggs, milk and vanilla well and then pour the mixture over the bread. Bake at 350° for 25-30 minutes or until light brown. Allow bread to sit for 10-15 minutes, top with syrup and serve.

*If using fresh peaches, marinate with sugar, to taste, for 30 minutes before adding to baking dish.

Bardstown

Settled in the late 1700's, Bardstown is Kentucky's second oldest city. Some of Kentucky's largest distilleries are here due to the high lime content in the local water supply. Visit the Oscar Getz Museum to see a confiscated copper still that belonged to George Washington.

Grits Cakes with Fresh Tomato Sauce

"A new twist on grits! We love them here."

Marsha Burton—The Inn At Woodhaven, Louisville

Grits Cakes:
  1 Tbsp. BUTTER
  1 med. ONION, chopped
  2 cups LOWFAT MILK
  1 1/2 cups QUICK GRITS
  1/3 cup grated PARMESAN CHEESE
  2 Tbsp. finely chopped BASIL
  1/4 tsp. SALT

Tomato Sauce:
  2 Tbsp. OLIVE OIL
  2 sm. RIPE TOMATOES, seeded
    and finely chopped
  1 Tbsp. finely chopped BASIL
  1/4 tsp. SALT
  1/4 tsp. PEPPER

Grease an 8-inch baking pan. In a medium saucepan, melt butter and sauté onion until browned. Add milk and heat to boiling. Slowly add grits, stirring constantly, until well-blended. Add Parmesan, basil and salt and continue to cook, stirring constantly until mixture is thick. Pour into baking pan and spread evenly. Cool to room temperature, then cover and refrigerate until firm (can be prepared the day before). In a large skillet, heat 1 tablespoon olive oil. Add tomatoes, basil, salt and pepper. Sauté tomatoes for 1 minute. Set aside to cool. When ready to serve, loosen edges of grits from pan with a knife and invert onto a baking sheet. Cut grits into 9 squares, then cut each square diagonally to make triangles. Brush tops with remaining tablespoonful of oil and broil until lightly browned. Serve grits topped with sauce or serve sauce on the side.

Serves 4.

Easy Breakfast Casserole

"This easy meal can be made even easier. Combine the ingredients the night before, refrigerate and bake in the morning for a great breakfast!"

Lynda Mays—Lexington

4-6 slices BREAD
1-1 1/2 lbs. BULK SAUSAGE
2 cups shredded SHARP
   CHEDDAR CHEESE
6 EGGS

2 cups MILK
1 tsp. DRY MUSTARD
1 tsp. SALT
Dash of PEPPER

Tear bread slices and use them to cover the bottom of a buttered 13 x 9 baking dish. Brown and drain sausage. Spoon sausage over bread then sprinkle with cheese. Beat together the remaining ingredients and pour over top of cheese. Bake at 350° for 35-45 minutes.

Cabin Grits Fritters

"This is my original recipe and one of my guests' favorites!"

JoAnn Young Bland—Coffee Tree Cabin Bed & Breakfast,
Bardstown

3/4 cup MILK
1 pkg. (1 oz.) INSTANT GRITS
1/2 cup chopped GREEN ONIONS (include stems and bulbs)
1/4 cup CHEDDAR CHEESE
1/4 cup MONTEREY JACK CHEESE
2 EGGS
2 dashes TABASCO®
SALT and PEPPER to taste
1 1/2 Tbsp. SELF-RISING FLOUR

Place milk in a microwaveable dish and heat for 2 minutes on high. Stir in the grits. Microwave 1 minute more. Add onions, cheeses and eggs and stir. Add remaining ingredients. Drop heaping tablespoons of mixture onto a hot, oiled griddle and brown lightly.

Makes 12 fritters.

Spoon Bread

"This tastes great when served with fried apples and sausage!"

Ann Childs—Shelbyville

1 cup BOILING WATER
1/2 cup CORNMEAL
1/2 cup MILK
1 1/2 tsp. BAKING POWDER

1/2 tsp. SALT
1 Tbsp. softened BUTTER
2 EGGS, well beaten
Fried SAUSAGE

In a large bowl, pour boiling water over the cornmeal. Beat in milk, baking powder, salt and butter. Blend in eggs. Pour mixture into a 1-quart buttered casserole dish and bake at 400° for 20-30 minutes. Spoon bread onto serving plates, add sausage and ***Fried Apples.***

Fried Apples

6 APPLES, sliced
2 tsp. BUTTER
1 cup WATER

1 cup SUGAR
CINNAMON to taste

In a large skillet, melt butter, add water and apple slices and cook until tender. Stir in sugar and cinnamon; cook on low heat until thickened.

Hashbrown Heaven

"This is our signature dish. We usually serve it on Sundays."

Ann Driver—Trinity Hills Farm Bed & Breakfast, Paducah

2 cups frozen HASHBROWNS, defrosted
1 cup shaved HAM
1 can (2.5 oz.) MUSHROOMS, drained
1/4 cup diced GREEN BELL PEPPER
2 cups grated COLBY JACK CHEESE
7 EGGS, beaten

2 cups MILK
1 Tbsp. BUTTER
  (squeeze type)
SALT and PEPPER,
  to taste

Preheat oven to 350°. Grease 2 pie plates. Beginning with a layer of hashbrowns, add layers of meat, vegetables and cheese to plates. Beat remaining ingredients together and pour over top of cheese. Bake 45-50 minutes or until firm in center.

Soups & Salads

Ale'd Potato Soup

"This makes a sublime first course or a captivating supper. The ale, ham and green onions add an appealing change of pace to the creamy potato-laden base."

Oldenberg Brewing Company—Fort Mitchell

3 Tbsp. BUTTER
3-4 oz. CANADIAN BACON
   or HAM, julienned
2 med. ONIONS, finely chopped
2 cups CHICKEN STOCK
1 1/2 cups GOLDEN ALE

1 tsp. dried THYME or DILL
5 med. POTATOES, julienned
2 cups HEAVY CREAM
SALT and PEPPER to taste
Minced PARSLEY
Chopped GREEN ONIONS

In a skillet, melt butter over medium heat. Fry bacon until lightly browned and crisp. Remove and set aside. Add onions to the skillet and sauté until wilted. Remove and set aside. Combine the stock, ale and thyme in a large Dutch oven and heat over medium-high heat. Add the potatoes, bacon and onions to the stock and bring the mixture to a slow boil. Cook until the potatoes are just tender (35-40 minutes). Remove from heat and slowly stir in the cream. Reheat just until bubbles begin to form around the edges. Remove from heat; season with salt and pepper. Garnish with parsley and green onion.

Serves 6.

Peggy's Winter Soup

"I like to develop my own gourmet recipes. This soup was inspired by heavy snow and winter's chill."

Peggy Hagan—Shelbyville

1-2 Tbsp. OLIVE OIL
1/4 cup finely diced ONION
2 cloves GARLIC, minced
1 cup VEGETABLE BROTH
1/2 lb. MUSHROOMS, sliced and stems chopped
1 Tbsp. chopped fresh PARSLEY
1 Tbsp. chopped fresh CILANTRO
1/2 cup CHAMPAGNE
1 can (15 oz.) GREAT NORTHERN BEANS, with liquid
1 dried THAI HOT PEPPER, crushed
4 oz. BLUE CHEESE, if desired
SALT to taste
VEGETABLE BROTH CUBES or GRANULES, to taste

In a large saucepan, heat oil; add onion and garlic and sauté until onion is translucent. Stir in vegetable broth, mushrooms, parsley, cilantro and champagne; mix well. Add beans and hot pepper. Crumble cheese and sprinkle into mixture. Season with salt and vegetable broth. Simmer for 15-20 minutes.

Serves 2.

Cream of Corn Soup

This recipe is from the Lincoln Heritage Trail Cook Book

Abraham Lincoln Birthplace National Historic Site—Hodgenville

1/2 Tbsp. chopped ONION
3 Tbsp. BUTTER
3 Tbsp. FLOUR
1 cup HOT WATER

1 cup CORN
2 cups MILK
Pinch of CELERY SALT
Dash of PEPPER

Brown onion in butter, add flour and mix. Add water and corn and cook until mixture thickens. Add remaining ingredients and bring to a boil. Serve hot.

Polish Barley Soup

"This is my German great-grandmother's recipe."

Jane Gaines—Henderson

5 qts. CHICKEN STOCK, divided
2-3 CARROTS, thinly sliced
2 lg. ONIONS, finely chopped
2 cups CELERY, thinly sliced
1-2 med. TURNIPS, diced
1 cup sliced MUSHROOMS

2 BAY LEAVES
1 stick BUTTER
2 cups BARLEY
SALT and PEPPER to taste
SOUR CREAM

In a large pot, combine 3 quarts chicken stock with all of the vegetables and one bay leaf. Simmer. In a separate pot, combine the remaining 2 quarts of chicken stock with butter. Bring to a boil, add barley and remaining bay leaf. Simmer until all liquid is absorbed and barley is tender. Remove bay leaves. Add barley to vegetables. Simmer and adjust seasoning. Before serving, add a dollop of sour cream to each bowl.

Abraham Lincoln Birthplace National Historic Site

In a memorial just south of Hodgenville, you can view the cabin site where the 16th U.S. president was born and lived for the first two-and-a-half years of his life.

Gumbo Soup

This recipe is from the Lincoln Heritage Trail Cook Book

Abraham Lincoln Birthplace National Historic Site—Hodgenville

1/2 lb. BEEF
1/4 lb. HAM
1 1/2 Tbsp. FLOUR
1 Tbsp. PARSLEY
1 qt. OKRA, cut small

1/2 gal. WATER
4 CLOVES
Pinch of ALLSPICE
PEPPER to taste
1 Tbsp. SASSAFRAS

In a large skillet, fry beef and ham until brown. Add flour, parsley, okra, water, cloves, allspice and pepper. Cook until meat is tender. Just before serving, add sassafras.

Minestrone Soup

*"My mother used to make this soup when we were kids.
This was her favorite recipe."*

Sandy Zimmerman—Jamestown

1 cup dried WHITE NAVY BEANS
3 qts. WATER
2 tsp. SALT
1 sm. head CABBAGE, sliced
3 CARROTS, pared and diced
2 WHITE TURNIPS, pared and diced
1 can (15 oz.) TOMATOES, undrained
1 Tbsp. OLIVE or SALAD OIL
1 Tbsp. BUTTER or MARGARINE
1 cup thinly sliced ONION
1 lg. TOMATO, peeled and chopped
1/2 cup chopped CELERY
2 Tbsp. chopped PARSLEY
1 clove GARLIC, crushed
SALT and PEPPER to taste
1 cup broken-up THIN SPAGHETTI
Grated PARMESAN CHEESE

On the day prior to serving, cover beans with cold water in a medium bowl and refrigerate covered, overnight. Drain beans and place in a 5-quart Dutch oven or soup kettle with water and salt. Heat to boiling, then reduce heat. Gently simmer, covered, for 1 hour. Add cabbage, carrots, turnips and canned tomatoes; cover and continue to cook for 30 minutes. In a medium skillet, heat oil and butter; add onion and sauté until tender and golden. Add chopped tomato, celery, parsley, garlic, salt and pepper; cook over low heat for 20 minutes. Combine with bean mixture and add spaghetti; cover and cook over low heat for 30 minutes, stirring occasionally. When serving, sprinkle with Parmesan.

Serves 8-10.

Potato Soup

"A friend from church gave this recipe to me. This is a good dish on a cold winter day."

Martha N. Robertson—Brandenburg

4 cups thinly sliced POTATOES
1 med. ONION, chopped
1 Tbsp. BUTTER
1 1/2 cups POTATO WATER

1 1/2 cups EVAPORATED MILK
SALT and PEPPER to taste
4-5 tsp. minced PARSLEY

In a large saucepan, cover potato slices and onion with water. Cook, covered, on medium heat for 15 minutes; drain, reserving 1 1/2 cups of potato water. In a large mixing bowl, coarsely mash potatoes. Add butter, potato water, milk, salt and pepper. Return mixture to saucepan and heat. If a thinner soup is desired, add more water. Garnish with a teaspoon of parsley for each serving.

> ### Cooking Utensils in Lincoln's Day
> *The average family had three cooking utensils: an iron tea kettle, a three-legged skillet with an iron lid, and an iron pot which hung from a crane in the fireplace.*

Quick & Easy Fruit Salad

"My family always suggests this dish for Easter dinner."

Mae Beshear—Somerset

1 can (15.25 oz.) PINEAPPLE CHUNKS
1 can (16 oz.) CHUNKY MIXED FRUIT
2 lg. BANANAS, sliced
1 pkg. (3 3/4 oz.) INSTANT VANILLA PUDDING
3 Tbsp. TANG®

Drain pineapple and mixed fruit, reserving pineapple juice. Place fruit in a medium mixing bowl. In a small bowl, combine juice, pudding mix and Tang and stir well. Pour dressing mixture over fruit; toss gently and chill.

Serves 4.

Summer Salad

"This recipe is great for summer cookouts. You can change the vegetables to whatever is in the garden and ready to use."

Patricia Tindall—Shelbyville

4 cups fresh BROCCOLI and CAULIFLOWER CROWNS
1/4 cup chopped RED ONION
1/4 cup RAISINS
8 slices BACON, cooked and crumbled
1/2 cup sliced ALMONDS, toasted
1/4 cup SUGAR
3/4 cup MAYONNAISE
2 Tbsp. VINEGAR

In a salad bowl, combine broccoli and cauliflower crowns with onion, raisins, bacon and almonds; toss gently to mix. In a small bowl, mix sugar, mayonnaise and vinegar; let stand for 15 minutes. Pour dressing over salad and toss gently to coat. Chill and serve.

Fort Knox

The 100-foot-square U.S. Bullion Depository on Gold Vault Road in Fort Knox holds a large portion of the U.S. gold reserve.

Cranberry Salad

"This is one of my favorite easy recipes."

Marie Cubine—Louisville

2 cups HOT WATER
2 sm. pkgs. (3 oz. ea.) CHERRY JELL-O®
1 can (6 oz.) frozen ORANGE JUICE
1 can (20 oz.) crushed PINEAPPLE, drained
1 can (16 oz.) WHOLE CRANBERRY SAUCE
1 cup chopped PECANS

In a medium bowl, mix hot water, Jello and juice together; stir until Jell-O is dissolved. Add pineapple, cranberry sauce and pecans. Stir well. Chill until firm.

Cold Vegetable Salad

"As a side dish for fish, my family prefers this recipe instead of coleslaw."

Mae Beshear—Somerset

1 can (15.25 oz.) SHOE PEG CORN, drained
1 can (14.5 oz.) FRENCH CUT GREEN BEANS, drained
1 can (15 oz.) TINY PEAS, drained
1 cup chopped CELERY
1/2 cup chopped ONION
1 GREEN BELL PEPPER, chopped
1 jar (4 oz.) PIMENTO, drained

Dressing:

2/3 cup RED WINE VINEGAR   3/4 cup SUGAR
1/4 cup VEGETABLE OIL   SALT and PEPPER to taste

In a large mixing bowl, mix all vegetables together. In a small saucepan, combine vinegar, oil, sugar, salt and pepper; bring to a boil. Pour dressing over vegetables, chill and serve.

German Potato Salad

Nan Plenge—Shepherdsville

6 slices BACON   6 med. POTATOES
1/4 cup FLOUR   1/2 ONION, diced
1 cup VINEGAR   SALT and PEPPER to taste
1 1/2 cups WATER   CELERY SEED to taste
1 1/2 cups SUGAR

Cut bacon into small pieces. Fry in skillet until well done but not too crisp. Add flour to bacon and drippings and lightly brown. Add vinegar, water and sugar. Let simmer for 30 minutes or more, stirring occasionally. Boil potatoes for about 20 minutes (do not overcook, potatoes should remain firm). Peel and slice potatoes into 1/4-inch slices. Place in a serving bowl and sprinkle with onion, salt, pepper and celery seeds. Pour warm bacon mixture over the top. Serve hot.

Serves 12.

Lobster & Wild Rice Salad

Marsha Burton—The Inn at Woodhaven, Louisville

20 ASPARAGUS SPEARS
2/3 cup WILD RICE
2 ORANGES, sectioned, juice reserved

Dressing:
   Reserved ORANGE JUICE
   1 Tbsp. WHITE WINE VINEGAR
   1/8 tsp. SALT
   1/2 cup WALNUT OIL
   1 med. CARROT, finely chopped
   1/2 cup chopped WALNUTS
   1 GREEN ONION, finely chopped
   2 Tbsp. snipped fresh MINT

MESCLUN GREENS (see below)
8 cooked LOBSTER CLAWS and 8 oz. cooked LOBSTER MEAT

Cook asparagus in a small amount of boiling salted water until tender—about 8 minutes. Chill. Cook rice for 40 minutes in 1 2/3 cups boiling salted water. Drain and cool to room temperature. Peel oranges and section over a bowl to catch the juice. Add vinegar and salt to orange juice. Using a wire whisk, slowly blend in walnut oil. Add carrot, walnuts, onion, mint and rice to juice mixture and blend well. Arrange greens and asparagus on salad plates and top with dressing. Arrange lobster claws and meat around salad and garnish with orange slices.

Serves 4.

About Mesclun

Mesclun (also called salad mix *and* gourmet salad mix*) is simply a potpourri of young small salad greens. It can be found in specialty produce markets and many supermarkets. Commonly included greens are arugula, dandelion, frisée, mizuma, oak leaf, mâche, radicchio and sorrel.*

Overnight Vegetable Salad

"This is a great salad for family picnics."

Mary Putman—Henderson

1 can (14.5 oz.) GREEN BEANS
1 can (14.5 oz.) FRENCH CUT GREEN BEANS
1 can (15.25 oz.) CORN
1 cup diced CELERY
1/2 cup diced GREEN BELL PEPPER
1 med. ONION, chopped
1 jar (2 oz.) diced PIMENTOS
1/2 cup WHITE VINEGAR
1 1/2 cups SUGAR
1/2 cup SALAD OIL
2 Tsp. WATER
1/2 tsp. PAPRIKA

Drain liquids from beans and corn. In a large glass or ceramic bowl, combine all of the vegetables. In a small bowl, combine vinegar, sugar, salad oil, water and paprika. Mix until sugar has dissolved. Pour mixture over vegetables and toss. Chill salad overnight, or for 24 hours. Drain before serving.

Did You Know?
Bibb lettuce was first grown in Frankfort in the 1850s.

Cherry Salad

"A delicious dish that I make especially for the holidays."

Edna Guthrie—Eubank

1/2-3/4 cup SUGAR
1/2 cup WATER
1 can (21 oz.) CHERRY PIE FILLING
1 box (6 oz.) CHERRY JELL-O®

1 can (20 oz.) crushed
PINEAPPLE, drained
1 cup COLA
1/2 cup chopped NUTS

Place sugar, water and pie filling in a saucepan and boil for five minutes, stirring often. Remove from heat and add the balance of ingredients. Pour mixture into a 2-2 1/2 quart glass casserole dish and chill.

Taco Salad

"My neighbor gave me this recipe. It is a family favorite."

Lauren Russell—Verona

1 lg. GROUND BEEF, browned
   and drained
1 pkg. TACO SEASONING MIX
1 head LETTUCE, shredded
1 can (15 oz.) KIDNEY BEANS,
   drained

1 lg. ONION, diced
4 med. TOMATOES,
   chopped
8 oz. CHEDDAR CHEESE,
   shredded

Dressing:
   1 bottle (8 oz.) THOUSAND ISLAND DRESSING
   1/3 cup SUGAR

1 bag TORTILLA CHIPS, crushed

Mix meat with taco seasoning mix, reserving 1 tablespoonful for dressing. Layer salad in a large bowl, beginning with lettuce, then adding layers of beef mixture, beans, onions, tomatoes and cheese. To make dressing, combine Thousand Island with reserved taco seasoning and sugar. When ready to serve, add crushed chips to salad and toss with dressing.

Salmon Salad

"I remember eating this as a very young child. My family has used this recipe for years and it is delicious!"

Margaret H. Moffett—Shelbyville

2 Tbsp. LEMON JUICE
2 cups canned SALMON, flaked
1/2 cup diced CELERY
1/2 cup diced PICKLES
1/4 tsp. SALT
1/2 cup MAYONNAISE

4 hard-boiled EGGS, finely
   chopped
1/2 cup chopped GREEN
   ONIONS
LETTUCE LEAVES
CRACKER CRUMBS

In a large mixing bowl, sprinkle lemon juice over salmon. Stir in next six ingredients, mixing well. Serve on lettuce leaves. Garnish with cracker crumbs.

Note: Tuna can be substituted for the salmon, if desired.

Main Dishes

Spicy Fried Chicken & Gravy

"I have had this recipe for years and make it quite often. It is a delicious dish."

Lynda Mays—Lexington

8 CHICKEN BREAST HALVES
1 1/4 cups FLOUR
3/4 cup finely crushed POTATO
    CHIPS
1 tsp. CHILI POWDER
1/2 tsp. PAPRIKA
1/8 tsp. GARLIC POWDER

PEPPER to taste
2 EGGS
1 Tbsp. WATER
1/2 cup MARGARINE
1 med. ONION, chopped
2 Tbsp. BUTTER
1 1/2 cups MILK

Skin and bone the chicken, then cut meat into small strips. In a medium mixing bowl, combine flour, chips and spices; mix well and set aside. In a shallow dish, combine eggs and water and beat until blended. Dip chicken strips in egg mixture and dredge in flour mixture; reserve remaining flour mixture. In a skillet, melt margarine over medium heat; add chicken and cook for 10 minutes on each side or until golden brown. Drain on paper towels and keep warm. Add onion and butter to skillet and sauté until onion is tender. Stir in 3 tablespoonfuls of reserved flour mixture and cook for 1 minute. Slowly add milk, stirring constantly until thickened. Serve as gravy with chicken.

Tuna Burgers

"My mother created this recipe and served it on Fridays when we were not supposed to eat meat dishes."

Sandy Zimmerman—Jamestown

2 Tbsp. MARGARINE	1 can (6.5 oz.) TUNA,
1/2 cup chopped ONION	drained and flaked
1/4 cup chopped CELERY	1 Tbsp. PARSLEY
1 clove GARLIC, minced	SALT and PEPPER to taste
4 slices WHOLE-WHEAT BREAD	1 EGG
1/3 cup MILK	1/4 cup dry BREAD CRUMBS

In a small skillet, melt 1 tablespoon of margarine. Add onion, celery and garlic and cook for 3 minutes or until crisp-tender. In a large mixing bowl, soak bread in milk for 5 minutes then break into small pieces. Add sautéed mixture, tuna, parsley, salt and pepper; mix well. Add egg and mix well. Shape into 4 patties and roll in bread crumbs to coat. Refrigerate for 2-3 hours before cooking (helps patties retain shape while frying). In a large skillet, melt remaining margarine and fry patties until brown on both sides.

Kentucky Kernel Meatloaf

Hodgson Mill, Inc.—Hopkinsville

1 ONION, chopped
1 stalk CELERY, chopped
4 or 5 MUSHROOMS, chopped
2 lbs. GROUND BEEF
1 cup KENTUCKY KERNEL® SEASONED FLOUR
1/2 cup MILK
2 EGGS

In a skillet, sauté chopped vegetables. In a bowl, combine ground beef with vegetables. Add and combine seasoned flour, milk and eggs. Form meatloaf and place in a loaf pan. Bake at 375° for approximately 60 minutes.

Serves 8.

Pork Chops with Lima Beans

"I made up this recipe one day when I was trying to find something to make for dinner."

Cookie E. Whortenbury—Smithfield

1/2 cup COOKING OIL	1 lg. ONION, sliced
6 PORK CHOPS	SALT and PEPPER to taste
1 cup BUTTERMILK	2 cans (15 oz. ea.) LIMA BEANS
2 cups FLOUR	2 cups WATER

In a large skillet, heat oil. Dip pork chops in buttermilk then dredge with flour to coat; place in skillet and fry until brown. Arrange pork chops in a baking dish then top with onion slices and season with salt and pepper. Pour lima beans (with liquids) over onions, add water and bake at 375° for 1 hour.

Hamburger & 3 Bean Bake

"This tastes best when made one day and served the next."

Ann Childs—Shelbyville

1/4 cup chopped BACON
1/2 lb. GROUND BEEF
1 sm. ONION, chopped

Sauce:
    1/4 cup SUGAR
    1/4 cup packed BROWN SUGAR
    1/2 tsp. DRY MUSTARD
    1/4 cup KETCHUP
1 cup PORK & BEANS, with liquid
1 cup KIDNEY BEANS, drained
1 cup PINTO BEANS, drained

In a large skillet, cook bacon then drain. Add beef and onion to the pan and brown. Drain again. In a medium mixing bowl, combine sugars, mustard and ketchup; stir until blended. Combine beans, beef mixture and sauce and pour into a casserole dish. Cover and bake for 1 hour in a 350° oven.

Murphy's 'n Chops

"My sister, Billie Wooters, created this recipe. 'Murphy' is a slang term for potatoes."

Mary Ann Jeffries—Evansville

7 med. POTATOES, peeled and sliced 1/2-inch thick
1 lg. ONION, sliced into rings
6 (1-inch thick) PORK CHOPS
SALT and PEPPER to taste
2 cans (10.75 oz. ea.) CREAM OF TOMATO SOUP
1 soup can WATER

Spray a 10 x 13 baking pan with cooking spray. Layer potatoes and onion slices twice then place pork chops on top. Season with salt and pepper. In a mixing bowl, mix both cans of soup with 1 can of water; stir well. Pour over the pork chops. Cover and bake at 350° for 1 1/2 hours. Uncover and brown for 10-20 minutes.

Did You Know?

The McCoys, of the notorious Hatfield and McCoy feud, lived in the rolling hills of eastern Kentucky. Their arch rivals the Hatfields, lived across the river in West Virginia.

Sautéed Chicken Livers

"I serve this over rice with cole slaw and stewed tomatoes."

Ann Childs—Shelbyville

4 Tbsp. BUTTER
1 lb. CHICKEN LIVERS
1 GREEN BELL PEPPER,
    sliced into thin strips
1 sm. ONION, diced

1 tsp. chopped PARSLEY
1 tsp. minced GARLIC
SALT and PEPPER to taste
1 Tbsp. WHITE WINE
Cooked RICE

In a large skillet, melt butter; add chicken livers, bell pepper, onion, parsley, garlic, salt and pepper. Cover and simmer on low heat until livers are almost done, then add wine. Stir and continue to cook until most of the liquid is absorbed.

Mom's
Chicken & Dumplin's

"My mother cooked in restaurants in our community for years. This recipe was one of the patrons' favorites."

Connie Fowler—Stanford

1 (4-5 lb.) STEWING HEN, cut-up
SALT to taste
1/4 cup BUTTER or MARGARINE
2-3 qts. WATER
1 can (14.5 oz.) CHICKEN BROTH

Dumplings:

5 cups ALL-PURPOSE FLOUR	**2 1/2 tsp. SALT**
1/2 tsp. BAKING SODA	**1/2 cup SHORTENING**
1 tsp. BAKING POWDER	**1 1/2 cups BUTTERMILK**

In a large pot, place chicken, salt and butter; add water to cover. Cook until chicken is tender. Cool and debone chicken, cutting meat into bite-size pieces. Reserve broth. In a mixing bowl, combine flour, baking soda, baking powder and salt. Cut in shortening, add buttermilk and 1 cup of reserved broth. Stir until well-blended. Place dough on a floured surface and knead lightly. Roll out to 1/4-inch thickness and cut into small strips. Bring remaining broth to a boil and drop in all dough strips, one at a time. DO NOT STIR. Reduce heat, cover and simmer for 15-20 minutes. Add chicken to the broth during the last 10 minutes of cooking. If dumplings begin to dry out before cooking time is finished, heat canned chicken broth to boiling point and pour over the dumplings; boil for an extra 5 minutes.

Serves 12.

Kentucky in Hollywood
Movies using a Kentucky backdrop include: "The Insider," "Coal Miner's Daughter," "In Country," "Fire Down Below" and classics like "The Kentuckians" and "Raintree County."

"Best Ham Ever"

"My sister-in-law makes the best country ham I have ever eaten. This is her recipe."

Margaret H. Moffett—Shelbyville

1 WHOLE HAM
VINEGAR
WATER

Place ham in a (non-aluminum) soup kettle. Mix a ratio of 1 1/2 cups vinegar to 1 gallon of water, making enough to cover ham completely. Let sit for 18 hours; remove ham and rinse well. In another kettle, cover ham with water and cook on low heat at 20 minutes per pound. Place ham in a large baking pan, baste with your choice of the following glazes and bake at 325° for 4 1/2 hours. Turn oven off and leave ham in oven overnight. Reheat ham before serving.

Apricot Glaze

1/4 cup APRICOT PRESERVES   **1 tsp. HORSERADISH**
1 Tbsp. CHILI SAUCE   **MUSTARD**
1/2 tsp. DRY MUSTARD

In a small bowl, combine all ingredients; mix well.

Sweet & Sour Glaze

1-1 1/2 cups packed BROWN SUGAR   1/4 cup DIJON MUSTARD

In a small bowl, combine ingredients; mix well.

Brown Sugar Glaze

1 cup KARO® CORN SYRUP   1/2 cup packed BROWN SUGAR

In a small bowl, combine ingredients; mix well.

Honey Glaze

1 cup HONEY   **1 1/2 sticks CINNAMON**
2 cups APPLE CIDER   **1/2 tsp. GINGER**
1 tsp. ALLSPICE   **1 tsp. ground CLOVES**

In a medium bowl, combine ingredients; mix well.

Salisbury Steak Deluxe

"I have always made this recipe for my family and they just love it!"

Louise Butts—Smithfield

1 can (10.75 oz.) CREAM OF
    MUSHROOM SOUP, undiluted
1 Tbsp. MUSTARD
2 tsp. WORCESTERSHIRE SAUCE
1 tsp. HORSERADISH
1 EGG
1/4 cup dry BREAD CRUMBS
1/4 cup finely chopped ONION

1/2 tsp. SALT
Dash of PEPPER
1 1/2 lbs. GROUND BEEF
1-2 Tbsp. COOKING OIL
1/2 cup WATER
2 Tbsp. chopped fresh
    PARSLEY

In a small bowl, combine soup, mustard, Worcestershire sauce and horseradish; blend well and set aside. In a large mixing bowl, lightly beat egg, then add bread crumbs, onion, salt, pepper and 1/4 cup of the soup mixture. Add beef and mix well. Shape into six patties. In a large skillet, heat oil, add beef patties and brown; drain. Combine remaining soup mixture with water and pour over patties. Cover and cook over low heat for 10-15 minutes or until meat is done. Remove and place patties on a serving platter. Spoon sauce over meat and sprinkle with parsley.

Serves 6.

Colonel Harland Sanders

The Colonel Harland Sanders Museum in the Kentucky Fried Chicken Headquarters in Louisville and the Colonel Harland Sanders Cafe and Museum in Corbin both display memorabilia from the life of this most beloved Kentucky gentleman. He is the only fast food franchiser honored with a bust in the state capitol. The cafe in Corbin is the original restaurant where Col. Sanders first served his fried chicken. The Colonel's kitchen, where he experimented with pressure frying and created the recipe for his fried chicken with 11 herbs and spices, is featured here.

 # Lincoln's Steak

This recipe is from the Lincoln Heritage Trail Cook Book

Abraham Lincoln Birthplace National Historic Site—Hodgenville

A favorite from Lincoln days was a **THICK STEAK** browned in a heavy skillet with plenty of **BUTTER,** then spread with **SALT** and **MUSTARD** and cooked over a low heat until very tender. The steak was then placed on a hot platter along with **chopped PICKLED WALNUTS.** Then, **1 cup** of **STRONG COFFEE** was added to the skillet, let boil one time and poured over the steak before serving.

Thanksgiving

The first official proclamation of Thanksgiving was made by President Lincoln in 1863, setting aside the last Thursday of November as a day of thanks and prayer.

Benedictine Sandwich

"This sandwich spread was named for Miss Jennie Benedict, the Louisville cateress who created it."

Carrie Fulkerson—Sonora

1 pkg. (8 oz.) CREAM
    CHEESE, softened
1/2 CUCUMBER, peeled
    and chopped
1 tsp. finely grated ONION

MAYONNAISE
SALT and PEPPER to taste
GREEN FOOD COLORING
BREAD SLICES

In a medium mixing bowl, combine cream cheese, cucumber and onion; beat at medium speed until blended. Add enough mayonnaise to moisten, season with salt and pepper. Add small amount of food coloring to make a very pale-green filling. Spread on bread slices and serve either open-faced or in crust-trimmed sandwiches.

Prospect
Pork & Beef Barbecue

"My mother, Lena Burchett Guffey, used this recipe for family get-togethers after church."

Lois G. Newton—Shelbyville

5 lbs. PORK ROAST
5 lbs. boneless CHUCK ROAST
1/4 cup VEGETABLE OIL
4 med. ONIONS, chopped
3 stalks CELERY, chopped
4 cans (15 oz. ea.) TOMATO SAUCE
2 sauce cans WATER
2 bottles (14 oz. ea.) KETCHUP
1/2 cup packed BROWN SUGAR
2 Tbsp. CHILI POWDER
Dash WORCESTERSHIRE SAUCE

Place both roasts in a large roasting pan. Add a small amount of water. Roast at 350° for 2 hours or until meat is tender and falls from bones. Remove from pan and set aside to cool. Skim fat from drippings and reserve 1 cup. In a large skillet, heat oil and sauté onions and celery. Add remaining ingredients; cover and simmer slowly for 1 hour. Add sliced meat and reserved cup of drippings to skillet mixture. Simmer, uncovered, for 1 hour. Stir often.

Mammoth Cave National Park
The park, established in 1941, lies in central Kentucky. It surrounds Mammoth Cave, part of the world's longest known cave system. Visitors can be guided through 12 miles of corridors on five levels in the cave which contains several lakes, rivers and waterfalls. Many rocks in the cave resemble flowers, trees and waterfalls. There are also many blind creatures living in the cave including beetles, crayfish, bats and a strange eyeless fish.

Kentucky Hot Brown

"This is my favorite dish to serve for luncheons. I've never found it on a menu anywhere except in Kentucky."

Jean N. Sageser Stodghill—Shelbyville

Cheese Sauce:
- 3 Tbsp. BUTTER, melted
- 1/4 lb. PROCESSED AMERICAN CHEESE, cubed
- 2 cups MILK
- 1/2 tsp. SALT
- 1/2 tsp. PEPPER
- 3 Tbsp. FLOUR

- 4-6 slices BREAD
- Cooked, sliced TURKEY or CHICKEN BREAST
- Cooked BACON or sliced HAM
- 2 med. TOMATOES, sliced

In a double-boiler or heavy skillet, mix all sauce ingredients. Cook until cheese is melted and mixture is smooth. Toast bread. Layer bread with sliced turkey or chicken and cover with cheese sauce. Add slices of bacon or ham and top with tomato slices. Just before serving, place on a baking sheet and heat thoroughly under broiler.

Wakefield-Scearce Galleries

Historic Science Hill, home of Wakefield-Scearce Galleries in Shebyville, is listed on the National Register of Historic Places. In 1825, the buildings, dating to the early 1790s were converted to a finishing school for young ladies. The school operated continuously for 114 years.

Stewed Chicken

"We raised chickens on our farm so we always had plenty."

Pauline Thomas—Shelbyville

- 1 CHICKEN, cut into serving pieces
- 2 stalks CELERY, chopped
- 1 sm. ONION, diced
- SALT and PEPPER to taste

In a large pot, cover chicken with water; add celery and onion. Cook on low heat until meat is tender. Add salt and pepper. Dumplings may be added to broth.

Pepper Encrusted Pork Tenderloin

Heidi Caravan—Mt. Washington

2 PORK TENDERLOINS
1/2 cup MANGO CHUTNEY
3 Tbsp. coarsely ground BLACK PEPPER
MANGO SAUCE

Rinse and trim tenderloins. Place on waxed paper. Spread half of the chutney over one side of the pork, sprinkle with half of the pepper. Turn tenderloins over and repeat with remaining chutney and pepper. Bake in greased baking dish at 375° for 20 minutes. Turn meat over and bake for 30 minutes longer or until meat thermometer registers 170°. Slice into rounds. Serve with *Mango Sauce* on the side.

Serves 8.

Mango Sauce

1 cup SOUR CREAM   **1/3 cup MANGO CHUTNEY**

Combine ingredients and blend.

Glazed Ham

Morris Bitzer—Kentucky Sweet Sorghum Association, Clinton

1 lg. HAM

Sauce:
 1/2 cup SORGHUM
 1/2 tsp. MUSTARD
 1/3 cup ORANGE JUICE
ORANGE SLICES
MARASCHINO CHERRIES, halved

Bake ham per your favorite method. Combine sauce ingredients and spread over ham during the last 15 minutes of baking. Arrange cherry halves on orange slices and secure them on ham with toothpicks.

Lasagne Casserole

"This recipe makes two casseroles. Leftovers freeze well."

Tammy Schmid—Louisville

2 lbs. GROUND BEEF
1 lb. BULK SAUSAGE
1 ONION, chopped
1 pkg. frozen chopped SPINACH, cooked and drained
1/2 tsp. OREGANO
1 lg. pkg (16 oz.) uncooked EGG NOODLES
1 lb. CHEDDAR CHEESE, grated
1 lb. MOZZARELLA CHEESE, grated
2 cans (10.75 oz. ea.) CREAM OF MUSHROOM SOUP
2 soup cans MILK
1 lg. can (15 oz.) TOMATO SAUCE
1/2 cup PARMESAN CHEESE
1 sm. can (2.3 oz.) sliced BLACK OLIVES

In a large skillet, fry beef, sausage and onion. Remove all drippings and add spinach and oregano. Set aside. Cook egg noodles according to package directions, drain and set aside. Combine cheddar and mozzarella cheeses, set aside. Combine soup and milk, set aside. In 2 (9 x 13) baking dishes, layer noodles, meat mixture and cheeses. Repeat layers. Pour half of the mushroom soup mixture over each dish. Pour 1/2 of the tomato sauce over each. Sprinkle tops with Parmesan cheese and black olives. Bake at 325° for 30 minutes (increase baking time to 60 minutes if casserole has been frozen).

Serves 24.

The Louisville Slugger Museum

The World's largest baseball bat (120 feet long, 68,000 lbs, hollow carbon steel) can be found at the entranceway to this museum. After viewing the museum, visitors can see bats being produced for today's players at Hillerich & Bradsby Company's manufacturing facility.

Kentucky Burgoo

The center of the burgoo universe is Owensboro. During Owensboro's International Bar-B-Q Festival each May, 1,500 gallons of burgoo is served by the cup or by the gallon.

1 lb. PORK SHOULDER
1 lb. VEAL SHANK
1 lb. BEEF SHANK or OX TAIL
2 lbs. MUTTON or LAMB
    BREAST
6 qts. WATER
1 tsp. dried SAGE
2 tsp. dried THYME
2 whole BAY LEAVES
2 dried RED PEPPER PODS
4 tsp. SALT
3/4 tsp. freshly ground
    BLACK PEPPER
1 (4 lb.) HEN, with giblets
2 cups chopped CABBAGE

1 lb. boiling POTATOES, peeled
    and sliced
1 lb. ONIONS, peeled and
    chopped
1/2 lb. CARROTS, peeled and
    chopped
2 cups blanched, peeled, seeded
    and chopped TOMATOES
1 cup LIMA BEANS
1 1/2 cups CORN
1 cup thinly sliced OKRA
1 1/2 Tbsp. WORCESTERSHIRE
    SAUCE
1/2 cup chopped fresh PARSLEY

Combine the pork, veal, beef and mutton in a 16-quart stockpot. Add water, sage, thyme, bay leaves, red pepper, salt and black pepper. Bring to a boil over high heat, reduce heat and simmer gently for 30 minutes. Add the hen and its giblets. Continue simmering gently for another 1 1/2 hours, or until all the meats are tender. Remove the meats and set aside to cool. Bone and chop all of the meat (or put it through the coarse blade of a food grinder—do not use a food processor.) Return the meat to the broth and add the cabbage, potatoes, onions, carrots and tomatoes. Simmer for 30 minutes and then add the lima beans. Cook at the barest simmer for 1 1/2 hours. Add the corn, okra and Worcestershire sauce and cook for an additional 30 minutes. Stir in the fresh parsley, add salt and pepper to taste.

Serves 16.

Note: Serve burgoo with a spicy potato salad that includes pickle relish, boiled eggs and mustard and don't forget a slice of bread for sopping up the juices.

Country-Style Ribs with Peaches

Juli Duvall—Louisville

4 lbs. COUNTRY-STYLE RIBS

Marinade:
  1 1/2 cups OIL
  3/4 cup SOY SAUCE
  1/2 cup VINEGAR
  1/4 cup WORCESTERSHIRE SAUCE
  1/3 cup ORANGE JUICE
  1 tsp. DRY MUSTARD
  1 Tbsp. coarsely ground BLACK PEPPER
  2 tsp. SALT
  2 Tbsp. chopped fresh PARSLEY
  2 cloves GARLIC, minced

HONEY

1 lg. can (16 oz.) sliced PEACHES

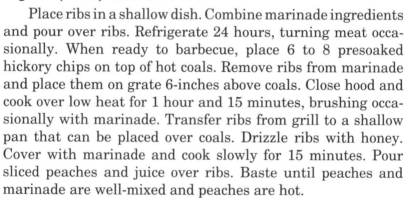

Place ribs in a shallow dish. Combine marinade ingredients and pour over ribs. Refrigerate 24 hours, turning meat occasionally. When ready to barbecue, place 6 to 8 presoaked hickory chips on top of hot coals. Remove ribs from marinade and place them on grate 6-inches above coals. Close hood and cook over low heat for 1 hour and 15 minutes, brushing occasionally with marinade. Transfer ribs from grill to a shallow pan that can be placed over coals. Drizzle ribs with honey. Cover with marinade and cook slowly for 15 minutes. Pour sliced peaches and juice over ribs. Baste until peaches and marinade are well-mixed and peaches are hot.

Did You Know?

The north-central Bluegrass region of Kentucky is known as "The Horse Capital of the World." Owensboro is known as "The Barbecue Capital of the World," and Bardstown is known as "The Bourbon Capital of the World." The Land between the Lakes in southeastern Kentucky was once known as "The Moonshine Capital of the World."

Side Dishes

Shucky Beans

"Also known as Leather Britches, this recipe is a favorite of Kentucky mountain people and very popular for their Thanksgiving and Christmas dinners. A bushel of green beans, dried, makes a gallon of the beans used in this recipe."

Delana Sue Trent—Mayking

1 qt. dried GREEN BEANS
1 cup dried GREAT NORTHERN BEANS
1/2 cup LARD
1 tsp. SALT
1 sm. chunk or 2 slices SALT BACON

Remove "strings" from green beans. Thread a large needle with crochet thread or twine. Pierce the center of a bean with the needle, pull thread through and tie a knot around the bean. Continue to thread beans, leaving space between each one. When string is complete, hang it in a dry place where air can circulate around the beans (they are best if dried in the sun). When beans are completely dry (they will rattle when touched and be yellow-brown in color); break beans from string and shuck. Place dried beans in freezer bags and freeze. To cook, place beans in a large saucepan of water and cook over medium heat for 1 hour. Drain and rinse. Place beans in another saucepan and add great northern beans, lard, salt and salt bacon. Cook until beans are tender.

Makes 3-4 quarts.

Baked or Deep-Fried Potato Puffs

"My mom taught me to make these the way she had been making them all my life. She didn't have a recipe, she just made them!"

Karen J. Burch—Frankfort

2 cups MASHED POTATOES
2 Tbsp. BUTTER
2 EGGS, beaten

1/2 cup CREAM
SALT and PEPPER to taste

In a medium mixing bowl, combine all ingredients and stir until blended. Form mixture into small balls. Bake at 400° until golden brown or deep-fry if you prefer.

The Frankfort Cemetery

A monument marks the graves of Daniel Boone and his wife, Rebecca, buried in this cemetery which overlooks downtown Frankfort. A black granite wall here bears the names of Kentuckians who have died defending their country from the War of 1812 through the Gulf War.

Hoppin' John

Senator Mitch McConnell—Washington, D.C.

2 cups BLACK-EYED PEAS
1/4 lb. BACON, chopped
2 sm. RED PEPPER PODS
2 cups uncooked WHITE RICE
SALT to taste

In a saucepan, cover peas with water. Add bacon and peppers to the saucepan. Simmer, covered, over low heat for 1 to 1 1/2 hours, or until peas are tender. Add rice and salt, cover, and cook over low heat, stirring frequently until rice is cooked. Add more water during cooking if necessary.

Serves 8.

Barn Raising Mashed Potatoes

"Kentuckians raise potatoes and serve them in many ways. This ageless recipe is a family favorite."

Doris Arnold—Frankfort

4 lg. POTATOES, peeled
  and chunked
1 pkg. (3 oz.) CREAM CHEESE,
  softened

3 Tbsp. BUTTER
MILK
SALT to taste

Boil potatoes until tender, then drain and place in a large mixing bowl. While still hot, mash, adding cream cheese, butter and enough milk to make the mixture creamy. Add salt to taste.

Note: Leftovers can be mixed with an egg, a small amount of flour and chopped onion, shaped into patties and fried to make potato cakes.

Did You Know?

In spite of the fact that most of the bourbon whiskey produced in the world is made in Kentucky, alcoholic beverages cannot be bought legally in seventy-five of Kentucky's counties.

Best Beets

"This is a dish my family always likes."

Louise Butts—Smithfield

3/4 cup SUGAR
2 tsp. CORNSTARCH
1/3 cup VINEGAR
1/3 cup WATER
1 tsp. DRY MUSTARD

1 tsp. ONION POWDER
4 cups sliced BEETS, cooked
3 Tbsp. BUTTER or MARGARINE
1/4 tsp. SALT
Dash of WHITE PEPPER

In a large saucepan, combine sugar and cornstarch. Add vinegar and water and bring to a boil. Add all remaining ingredients. Reduce heat and simmer until thoroughly heated.

Serves 6-8.

Grandmother's Chow-Chow

"Chow-chow is usually served with meats or used in potato or tuna salads. This is a family recipe."

Dottie Tyler—Smithfield

1 peck GREEN TOMATOES
2 stalks CELERY
2 med. heads CABBAGE
10 med. ONIONS
10 RED or GREEN BELL PEPPERS
1/2 cup SALT
6 cups VINEGAR
10 cups SUGAR
3 Tbsp. CELERY SEEDS
3 Tbsp. MUSTARD SEEDS

In a food processor or blender, grind all vegetables. In a large mixing bowl, combine vegetables with salt. Allow to stand overnight. Drain off liquid. In a large saucepan, combine vinegar, sugar, celery and mustard seeds; bring to a boil. Add vegetable mixture, bring to a boil again and cook until vegetables are translucent. Pour into sterilized pint jars and seal.

Yields 16 -18 pints.

Kentucky's Covered Bridges

More than 400 "kissing bridges" covered Kentucky's creeks and rivers around the turn of the century. Today, however, only 13 of these historic gems remain.

Mom's "Good Dish"

"This was my mother's recipe; she made it as an 'extra' dish to help feed 12 children."

Vera Caudill—Whitesburg

1 sm. head CABBAGE, chopped
1 can (15.25 oz.) WHOLE KERNEL CORN, drained
1 can (16 oz.) TOMATOES, with juice
2-3 BANANA PEPPERS, diced
SALT, SEASONED SALT, and PEPPER to taste

In a large saucepan, combine all ingredients. Cook on medium heat until cabbage is tender.

Dr. Bruce's
Twice-Baked Spuds

*"My brother created this recipe. He is known as
'the cook' in our family."*

Kelly A. Schweitzer—Shelbyville

6 lg. BAKING POTATOES, unpeeled
10-12 strips BACON
1/2 cup chopped ONION
GARLIC SALT to taste
2 cups grated SHARP CHEDDAR CHEESE
1 bottle (8 oz.) RANCH DRESSING
PAPRIKA
PARSLEY

Bake potatoes until tender. Cut in half lengthwise and let cool completely. In a skillet, cook bacon until crisp, reserving 2 tablespoonfuls of bacon drippings. Crumble bacon and set aside. In skillet, with remaining bacon drippings, sauté onions until translucent. Drain and set aside. Hollow out potato halves with a large serving spoon, leaving enough potato in skins to retain shape. In a large mixing bowl, combine potatoes, bacon, onion, garlic salt and 1 cup of the cheese. Beat on medium speed, gradually adding dressing until desired consistency is reached. Re-stuff potato skins with mixture and sprinkle tops with remaining cheese. Garnish with paprika and parsley. Place stuffed skins on a lightly greased cookie sheet and bake at 350° for 20-25 minutes.

Lexington

One of the nation's leading trading centers for tobacco, bluegrass seed and white barley, the Lexington area is also a leading market for racehorses. Founded in 1775, Lexington was named for the opening battle of the Revolutionary War at Lexington, MA. This city served as the state capital in 1792 and 1793.

Latitia's
Cornbread Dressing

"My momma raised ten children and three grandchildren.
She used this recipe whenever she had leftover cornbread."

Mary Reynolds—Eubank

4 cups crumbled CORNBREAD
1 med. ONION, chopped
SALT and PEPPER to taste
Bacon, pork, or chicken
   PAN DRIPPINGS

SAGE to taste
2 EGGS, beaten
1/4 cup BUTTER
MILK

Place cornbread in a bowl and add the onion, salt, pepper and sage. Mix well. In a skillet, heat enough pan drippings to cover the bottom. When drippings are hot, add the cornbread mixture and stir until coated. Lower heat and add the eggs and butter, stirring constantly. Add milk until mixture is like a moist dressing. Cook on low for 5-10 minutes. Make a pan of gravy to pour over the dressing.

Grandma Stevens'
Rice & Mushrooms

"Sunday lunch is a weekly event at my mother-in-law's (Grandma Stevens) house that has lasted through several generations. She always makes a family feast that is 'fit for a king' with a country-style entree and ten to twelve side dishes. She is truly one of the great Kentucky country cooks."

John Muenks—Shelbyville

1 cup RICE
1 stick BUTTER
1 lg. ONION, diced

1 can (10.75 oz.) BEEF CONSOMMÉ
1 can WATER
1 can (4.5 oz.) sliced MUSHROOMS

In a large skillet, combine rice, butter and onion and fry until brown. In a casserole dish, combine consommé, water and mushrooms; add rice mixture. Bake, uncovered, at 325° until rice swells, then cover and cook 1 hour longer.

Hush Puppies *

"This is a favorite Kentucky side dish."

Ann Peek—Fredonia

2 lg. SWEET ONIONS, finely grated
1 cup SELF-RISING FLOUR
1 cup SELF-RISING CORNMEAL
1 EGG, beaten
2 Tbsp. SUGAR
1 Tbsp. PARSLEY FLAKES
1/2 tsp. GARLIC POWDER

In a medium mixing bowl, combine all ingredients. Heat oil in a large heavy skillet or deep fryer. Carefully drop tablespoonfuls of batter into oil and fry until golden brown.

The Bluegrass State

The Bluegrass Region covers the north-central part of the state, with the Ohio River bordering the north and west areas. Kentucky's largest cities, most of its horse farms and much of its manufacturing are in the Bluegrass Region.

Tomato Pie

Tammy Outlaw—Livermore

1 med. ONION, chopped
1 med. TOMATO, diced
1 (9-inch) deep-dish baked PIE SHELL
1 lb. BACON, cooked
1 cup shredded MOZZARELLA CHEESE
1 cup shredded CHEDDAR CHEESE
1 cup MIRACLE WHIP® SALAD DRESSING

Preheat oven to 350°. Layer onions and tomatoes in pie shell; crumble bacon on top. In a medium mixing bowl, mix cheeses and salad dressing together. Pour cheese mixture into pie shell, covering all of the bacon and spreading to the edges. Bake at 350° until cheese melts and is golden brown. Serve hot or cold.

Shirley's Macaroni & Cheese

"This is my son and son-in-law's favorite side dish. It is also a great main dish served with a salad or green vegetable. When done, it resembles a soufflé."

Shirley Roberts Louden—Smithfield

1 cup ELBOW or SHELL MACARONI
1 1/2 sticks MARGARINE
5-6 slices day-old BREAD
6 slices VELVEETA®
SALT and PEPPER to taste
1 EGG
2 cups EVAPORATED MILK

Prepare macaroni according to package instructions, drain. In a saucepan, melt 1 stick of margarine. Tear bread into small pieces and toss with melted margarine until well-coated. Butter a 2-quart casserole dish. Layer 1/2 of the macaroni, 4 pats of margarine and 3 slices of Velveeta. Season with salt and pepper. Repeat layer, then cover top with buttered bread pieces. In a small mixing bowl, beat egg and milk together. Pour over top of bread. Bake at 350° for 30 minutes or until bubbly.

Fried Green Tomatoes

"A saga of fried food, Kentucky style, would be incomplete without mention of fried green tomatoes."

Carrie Fulkerson—Sonora

6 GREEN TOMATOES
SALT and PEPPER to taste
SUGAR

CORNMEAL
BACON DRIPPINGS
or OIL

Slice firm green tomatoes into 1/4 to 1/2-inch thick slices. Sprinkle with salt, pepper and sugar. Dip each slice in cornmeal to coat. In a large skillet, heat bacon drippings or oil; add tomato slices. Fry until brown, turn and brown the other side.

Stuffed Eggplant

"This recipe is over 80 years old! It has been featured in over 50 publications."

Mike Stone—Old Stone Inn, Simpsonville

1 lg. EGGPLANT
2 cups WATER
1/2 tsp. SALT
1 Tbsp. BUTTER
1/4 cup chopped ONION
1 tsp. WORCESTERSHIRE SAUCE
1 Tbsp. chopped PARSLEY
1 can (10.75 oz.) CREAM OF MUSHROOM SOUP
1 cup (24) finely crushed RITZ® CRACKERS

Preheat oven to 375°. Halve eggplant and scoop out to within 1/2-inch of skin. Set hulls aside. Dice eggplant meat into 1/4-inch pieces. In a saucepan, place eggplant, 1/2 cup water and salt and cook over medium heat until tender. Drain in a colander. In a skillet, melt butter, add onion and sauté until translucent. In a large mixing bowl, combine onion, eggplant and Worcestershire sauce. Add parsley, soup and cracker crumbs until thickened. Stuff eggplant hulls with mixture and sprinkle tops with extra cracker crumbs. Pour 1 1/2 cups of water into a baking pan. Arrange stuffed eggplants in pan. Bake at 375° for 1 hour.

Bell County
• *In Middlesboro, visit the "Coal House", built of 42 tons of bituminous coal.*
• *U.S. Hwy. 25E—Take the twin-bore 4,600 foot tunnels which pass under Cumberland Gap.*
• *The Cumberland Gap National Historical Park—Breathtaking view overlooking 3 states at Pinnacle Overlook.*
• *Pine Mountain State Resort Park—See Chained Rock, a huge chain is anchored to a boulder and seems to be holding the rock in place—1,000 feet over the city of Pineville!*

Broccoli Casserole

"This is a recipe my mother often used for Sunday dinners."

Lois G. Newton—Shelbyville

1 cup crushed SNACK CRACKERS
2 cups chopped BROCCOLI
1 EGG
1 can (15 OZ.) CREAM-STYLE CORN
 stick MARGARINE, softened

In a buttered casserole dish, place 1/2 of the cracker crumbs. Place broccoli on top of the crackers. In a small mixing bowl, beat egg, corn and 3/4 of the margarine together. Pour over broccoli. Top with the remaining cracker crumbs and dot with margarine. Bake at 350° for 45 minutes.

Old-Fashioned Wilted Lettuce

"This is a family favorite I have made so many times I no longer look at the recipe! Both my grandmother and my mother made this dish. It is delicious with fried potatoes or brown beans."

Margaret H. Moffett—Shelbyville

8 slices BACON
1 head LETTUCE, torn
3-5 GREEN ONIONS, chopped

SALT and PEPPER to taste
1/4 cup VINEGAR
1/4 cup SUGAR

In a large skillet, cook bacon until crisp, then drain and crumble. Reserve drippings. Place lettuce in a large salad bowl; add onions, salt and pepper and toss lightly. In the skillet, reheat bacon drippings. Add vinegar and sugar and stir until blended. Heat mixture to scalding and pour over lettuce. Add bacon and serve while still hot.

Did You Know?

In technical terms "Kentucky has more running water than any other state except Alaska!"

Granny's Tomato Dumplings

"Here in Kentucky, we eat Granny Mary June Roberts' tomato dumplings as a side dish, served with creamed potatoes and salmon croquettes—a typical southern meal."

Shirley Roberts Louden—Smithfield

1 qt. frozen TOMATOES or 2 cans (16 oz. ea.) diced TOMATOES
1 stick MARGARINE or BUTTER
SALT to taste
1 slice day-old BREAD
4-5 slices fresh BREAD
3/4 cup SUGAR

In a heavy, nonstick saucepan, combine tomatoes, margarine and salt. If using frozen tomatoes, cover and cook on low until thawed. Add a slice of day-old bread to thicken. Tear small pieces of fresh bread and roll between fingers to make little "dumplings" and add to tomato mixture. Cook on low heat until mixture is almost clear. Stir in sugar.

Harvard Beets

"This was my grandmother Lilly May Youngman's recipe. She always made this dish when we came to visit because she knew it was my favorite."

Jennie Early—Reynold's Aluminum Supply Co., Shelbyville

2 Tbsp. BUTTER
1 Tbsp. FLOUR
1/2 cup SUGAR
1/2 tsp. SALT
1/4 cup VINEGAR
1/4 cup BEET JUICE
or WATER
2 cups cooked sliced BEETS, drained

In a small saucepan, melt butter and stir in flour. Gradually add sugar, salt, vinegar and beet juice or water. Cook until clear, stirring constantly. Add beets and heat thoroughly.

Jewell's Potato Casserole

"This is a favorite at family gatherings."

Kathy Jo King—Shelbyville

1/2 stick BUTTER
1 sm. ONION, chopped
1 stalk CELERY, chopped
1 lb. frozen SOUTHERN-STYLE HASH BROWNS, partially thawed
1 can (10.75 oz.) CREAM OF MUSHROOM SOUP
1 can (10.75 oz.) CREAM OF CHICKEN SOUP
1 ctn. (8 oz.) SOUR CREAM
1-1 1/2 cups grated SHARP CHEDDAR CHEESE

Melt butter in a small skillet. Add onion and celery and sauté until onion is translucent. In a large mixing bowl, combine onion mixture with hash browns, soups and sour cream; mix well. Pour mixture into a 9 x 13 baking dish and sprinkle top with cheese. Bake at 350° for 1 hour.

Cheese Pudding

"In 1954, when President Eisenhower was served this dish at the Hodgenville Women's Club, he asked for a second helping and for the recipe!"

Carrie Fulkerson—Sonora

1 cup crushed SODA CRACKERS
2 cups WHITE SAUCE
1/2 lb. AMERICAN CHEESE, grated
4 hard-boiled EGGS, chopped
1 can (7 oz.) PIMENTOS, chopped
BUTTERED CRUMBS

In a bowl, combine cracker crumbs with white sauce and stir with fork until all crumbs are moistened. (You may need to add a small amount of milk to ensure all crumbs are moistened.) Place a layer of crumbs in a buttered casserole dish and add a layer of cheese, a layer of eggs and a layer of pimentos. Repeat layers. Top with buttered crumbs. Bake at 350° for 30 minutes.

Bourbon Marinade

Tammy Schmid—Louisville

1/4 cup VINEGAR
3 Tbsp. MAPLE SYRUP
1/4 cup DIJON MUSTARD
2 tsp. HOT SAUCE
2 tsp. WORCESTERSHIRE SAUCE

2 Tbsp. BOURBON
1/3 cup OLIVE OIL
4 cloves GARLIC, minced
2 tsp. ITALIAN SEASONING
BLEND

In a bowl, combine all ingredients thoroughly. Place meat (chicken or steak) in a single layer in a large shallow dish. Pour marinade over top and cover with plastic wrap. Marinate overnight in refrigerator, turning meat over at least once.

Makes enough marinade for 4 chicken breasts or 4 steaks.

Kentucky Bourbon Whiskey

Bourbon was first produced in Kentucky by pioneers. It gets its distinctive taste from being aged in charred oak barrels. The Oscar Getz Museum of Whiskey History in Bardstown exhibits include an 1854 E. C. Booz bottle, the brand from which the word "booze" originated.

Homemade Bar-B-Q Sauce

Ann Peek—Fredonia

4 cups SUGAR
1/2 cup ALL-PURPOSE FLOUR
2 tsp. BLACK PEPPER
1 tsp. RED PEPPER
1 tsp. SALT

2 cups MUSTARD
2 1/2 cups KETCHUP
1 cup WATER
5 cups VINEGAR
2 sticks MARGARINE

In a soup kettle, mix the first 5 ingredients together and stir until well-mixed. Add remaining ingredients and cook over low heat until margarine melts.

Makes 1 gallon.

Big John's BBQ Sauce

"Use this sauce on meat to be roasted, broiled or barbecued. It's also a great marinade and tenderizer!"

John Outlaw—Livermore

12 LEMONS
1 gal. WORCESTERSHIRE SAUCE
1/2 gal. VINEGAR
1 box (1 lb.) BROWN SUGAR

1 can (12 oz.) BEER
1 bottle (24 oz.) PANCAKE
    SYRUP
1 cup HOT SAUCE

Press down and roll lemons on a hard surface. Cut in half and squeeze juice into a large soup kettle. Add lemon peels and remaining ingredients. Stir well and then simmer for 20 minutes. Store in a sealed container or freeze for future use.

Scalloped Eggplant

"An unusual and very tasty vegetable dish."

Marie Cubine—Louisville

1 lg. EGGPLANT, peeled and diced
1/3 cup MILK
1 can (10.75 oz.) CREAM OF CHICKEN SOUP
1 EGG, slightly beaten
1/2 cup chopped ONION
1 cup shredded SHARP AMERICAN CHEESE
1 cup CRACKER CRUMBS
2 tbsp. MARGARINE or BUTTER, melted

In a medium saucepan, cook eggplant in boiling, salted water for 6-8 minutes or until tender; drain. In a medium mixing bowl, gradually stir milk into soup then blend in egg. Add eggplant, onion, cheese and 3/4 cup of the cracker crumbs. Toss lightly to mix. Pour mixture into a greased 10 x 6 baking dish. Finely crush remaining cracker crumbs. In a small bowl, combine cracker crumbs with butter and toss lightly. Sprinkle over top of mixture. Bake at 350° for 20 minutes.

Serves 6-8.

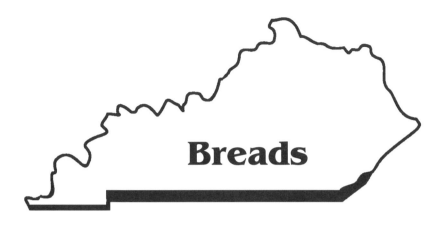

Breads

Blue Ribbon * Orange-Nut Bread

"This recipe has won a lot of Blue Ribbons at Kentucky county fairs."

Joan F. Jacobs—Frankfort

4 1/2 cups ALL-PURPOSE FLOUR
1 3/4 cups SUGAR
4 tsp. BAKING POWDER
1 tsp. BAKING SODA
1 1/2 tsp. SALT
1 1/2 cups chopped WALNUTS
2 Tbsp. grated ORANGE PEEL
2 EGGS
1 cup MILK
1 cup ORANGE JUICE
1/4 cup BUTTER, melted

In a large mixing bowl, combine flour, sugar, baking powder, baking soda and salt. Stir in nuts and grated orange peel. In a small bowl, beat eggs, milk, juice and butter until smooth. Stir into dry ingredients and mix until just moistened. Pour batter into 2 greased loaf pans. Bake at 350° for 50-60 minutes or until toothpick inserted in center comes out clean. Cool in pans for 10 minutes then remove and place on wire racks.

Corn Fritters

"This is a favorite at Old Stone Inn and included in every basket of bread we serve!"

Mike Stone—Old Stone Inn, Simpsonville

3/4 cup ALL-PURPOSE FLOUR
2 Tbsp. BAKING POWDER
1 tsp. SUGAR
1/2 tsp. SALT
1 EGG, beaten

1/2 cup MILK
2 cups CORN
OIL
POWDERED SUGAR

In a large mixing bowl, sift first four ingredients together. In a small bowl, combine egg, milk and corn then add to dry ingredients mixing until flour is moistened. Carefully drop teaspoonfuls of batter into deep, hot oil (375°). Fry 3-4 minutes or until golden brown and drain on paper towels. Dust with sifted powdered sugar. Serve warm.

Makes 50 fritters.

Grandma's Yeast Rolls

"This is a special family recipe."

Donna Marston—Frankfort

1/2 cup WATER
1/4 cup OIL
1/2 cup SUGAR
1 EGG, beaten

1 pkg. ACTIVE DRY YEAST
1/2 cup COLD WATER
3 cups unsifted FLOUR
3/4 tsp. SALT

In a medium saucepan, bring water to a boil. Add oil and sugar and stir until dissolved. Allow to cool then add egg. In a small bowl, dissolve yeast in cold water. Add to sugar mixture. Stir in flour and let rise in a warm place until doubled in bulk. Punch down and roll to 1/2-inch thickness. Use round cookie cutter to cut out rolls. Place rolls in a greased baking dish and let rise until doubled in bulk. Bake at 350° for 10-15 minutes.

Grandma's Sorghum Molasses Raisin Bread

"My aunt gave me this recipe 35 years ago. It was her grandmother's. It takes a lot of time and effort to make, but is well worth it."

Joan F. Jacobs—Frankfort

2 cups hot scalded MILK
2 Tbsp. melted SHORTENING
1/4 cup MOLASSES
1 pkg. ACTIVE DRY YEAST

3/4 cup RAISINS
1 tsp. CINNAMON
1 1/2 tsp. SALT
6 cups FLOUR

In a large mixing bowl, combine milk, shortening and molasses; allow to cool until lukewarm. Add yeast and let stand 5 minutes. Stir in raisins, cinnamon and salt. Add flour, a small amount at a time, mixing well after each addition until a stiff dough forms. Knead on a lightly floured board until smooth and elastic. Cover with a warm, damp cloth and let rise in a warm place until doubled in bulk. Punch down; let rise again until doubled in bulk. Form dough into three loaves and place in well-greased loaf pans. Cover and let rise again until doubled in bulk. Bake at 400° for 45 minutes or until golden brown.

Indian Bean Bread

This recipe is from the Lincoln Heritage Trail Cook Book

Abraham Lincoln Birthplace National Historic Site—Hodgenville

1/2 cup cooked BEANS
1 cup CORNMEAL

Pot of BOILING WATER

Mix beans and cornmeal together, adding enough water to moisten mixture until it holds together. Drop into boiling water and cook (as dumplings). This mixture was also wrapped in corn husks or large tree leaves, tied with a stout reed and then dropped into boiling water.

Grandmother's Biscuits

"I stood on a chair beside my grandmother when I was a child and learned how to make these biscuits."

Mary Osborne—Osborne's of Cabin Hollow Bed and Breakfast,
Somerset

2 cups SELF-RISING FLOUR
1/4-1/2 cup CRISCO®
1/4 tsp. SALT
1/4 tsp. BAKING POWDER
3/4 cup MILK

Preheat oven to 400°. Place flour in a mixing bowl and make a well in the center. Add shortening, salt and baking powder to well and then cut in. Add milk and mix until dough leaves sides of bowl clean. Turn out onto a floured surface and knead gently 10 times. Roll dough out to about 1/2-inch thickness and cut out biscuits. Place biscuits on a greased baking sheet. Bake for 12 minutes or until golden brown.

Makes 12-16 biscuits.

Fig-Strawberry Preserves

"Absolutely delicious!"

Susan Wise—Frankfort

3 cups mashed FIGS
1 pkg. (6 oz.) STRAWBERRY GELATIN
3 cups SUGAR

In a large saucepan, combine figs, gelatin and sugar. Mix well. Bring mixture to a boil over medium heat and boil for 3 minutes, stirring occasionally. Pour mixture into sterilized canning jars and seal with paraffin wax or seal and process in boiling water bath for 10 minutes.

Makes 3 pints.

Blueberry Streusel Muffins

Shelby Caravan—Mt. Washington

1 cup MILK
1/4 cup OIL
1/2 tsp. VANILLA
1 EGG
2 1/4 cups FLOUR
1/3 cup SUGAR
1 Tbsp. BAKING POWDER

1/2 tsp. SALT
1 cup frozen BLUEBERRIES, thawed
2 Tbsp. BROWN SUGAR
2 Tbsp. BUTTER, softened
1/4 tsp. CINNAMON

Heat oven to 400°. Grease bottoms only of 12 large muffin cups. Beat milk, oil, vanilla and egg together. Stir in 2 cups flour, sugar, baking powder and salt until just moistened. Gently fold in blueberries. Pour batter into muffin cups. In a small bowl, combine 1/4 cup flour, brown sugar, butter and cinnamon. Sprinkle over muffin tops and bake for 20 to 25 minutes.

Land Between the Lakes

This National Recreation Area lies between Barkley and Kentucky lakes in western Kentucky and Tennessee. This area provides more than 200 miles of hiking, mountain biking and horseback riding trails as well as fishing, boating, hunting and camping.

Persimmon Bread

Tom and Nancy Evans—Kentucky Nut Growers Assn., Henderson

1 cup PERSIMMON PULP
1/2 tsp. BAKING SODA
1/2 cup MARGARINE, softened
1 cup SUGAR
2 EGGS, beaten

1/2 cup chopped NUTS
1/2 cup RAISINS
2 cups FLOUR
3 tsp. BAKING POWDER
1/2 tsp. SALT

Combine all ingredients and mix well. Pour into 3 greased and floured small loaf pans. Bake at 350° for 45 minutes.

Fried Cornbread

"This bread was served with noon or evening meals. It was fried just right, in the old iron skillet."

Lynn Green—Waddy

2/3 cup YELLOW CORNMEAL
1 cup + 2 Tbsp. WATER

1/2 tsp. SALT
LARD or OIL

In a mixing bowl, combine cornmeal, water and salt and mix well. Pour mixture into a saucepan and boil for 3 minutes or until slightly thickened. In a skillet, heat lard. Spoon cornmeal mixture into the skillet, making 4 patties. Fry until golden brown on both sides.

Bowling Green

Visit the National Corvette Museum across the street from the General Motors Corvette Assembly Plant, to see an original Corvette from 1953, and the 1 millionth Corvette produced. The Kentucky Museum and Library at Western Kentucky University are also located in this southern Kentucky cultural center.

Honey-Pepper Jelly

Kathryn Bale—Frankfort

1 1/2 cups finely chopped RED BELL PEPPER
1 (1-inch long) TABASCO PEPPER, ground
1 1/3 cups VINEGAR
3 cups HONEY
1 pkg. powdered PECTIN

In a medium saucepan, bring peppers and vinegar to a full boil until foam drops. Add honey and bring to a boil again. Boil for 1 minute and then set aside for 20 minutes. Bring mixture to a boil again for 1 minute, add pectin and boil hard for 1 minute longer. Pour into five (1 cup) sterilized jars. Clean jar rims and screw caps on tightly. Invert for 10 minutes to seal.

Ma Stanley's Fried Biscuits

"My grandma Stanley liked to experiment when she was cooking. This is one of her recipes that has endured for over 50 years."

Teresa K. Ridgway—Shelbyville

1 cup POWDERED MILK
1/2 cup SUGAR
2 Tbsp. YEAST

2 Tbsp. OIL
2 cups HOT WATER
SELF-RISING FLOUR

Combine milk, sugar and yeast, then add oil and water. Mix well. Add flour until dough reaches a rolling consistency. Roll dough out to 1/2-inch thickness and cut out biscuits with biscuit cutter. Let rise (or freeze for later use). Fry on both sides until golden brown.

Banana-Nut Bread

"This bread freezes well."

Michael Schmid—Louisville

1 3/4 cups FLOUR
1/2 cup SUGAR
1/4 cup packed BROWN SUGAR
2 tsp. BAKING POWDER
1/2 tsp. BAKING SODA
Pinch SALT
1/2 tsp. CINNAMON
3 ripe BANANAS, mashed
1/3 cup BUTTER FLAVOR CRISCO®
2 Tbsp. MILK
2 EGGS, beaten
1/3 cup chopped NUTS
1/4 cup CINNAMON-SUGAR MIXTURE

In a large bowl, combine flour, sugars, baking powder, baking soda, salt and cinnamon. Add bananas and shortening. Mix well, then add milk and eggs. Fold in nuts. Pour into a greased and floured loaf pan. Sprinkle top with cinnamon sugar. Bake at 350° for about 60 minutes.

Carolyn's Monkey Bread

"You will always find this bread at our family reunions. It was my grandmother's recipe and remains a family favorite through three generations."

Teresa K. Ridgway—Shelbyville

1 cup MILK
1/2 cup BUTTER
1/4 cup SUGAR
1 tsp. SALT

1 pkg. ACTIVE DRY YEAST
3 1/2 cups ALL-PURPOSE FLOUR
Melted BUTTER

Combine milk, 1/2 cup butter, sugar and salt in a saucepan. Heat until butter melts. Cool to lukewarm, add yeast and stir until dissolved. Place flour in a large mixing bowl and add milk mixture. Stir until well-blended. Cover and let rise in a warm dry place, free from drafts, for about 1 1/2 hours or until doubled in size. Roll dough out into 1 1/2 inch balls. Dip each ball in melted butter. Layer balls of dough in a 10-inch (1-piece) tube pan. Cover with a dish towel and let rise about 45 minutes or until doubled in size. Bake at 375° for 35 minutes. Cool in pan about 10 minutes, then turn upside down onto serving dish.

Did You Know?

The traffic signal was invented by Garrett Morgan, a Paris, Kentucky native. This famous African-American inventor also developed a gas mask.

Short'nin' Bread

This recipe is from the Lincoln Heritage Trail Cook Book

Abraham Lincoln Birthplace National Historic Site—Hodgenville

1 stick BUTTER
1/4 cup LIGHT BROWN SUGAR

1 1/2 cups FLOUR

Mix butter with sugar. Add flour and mix well. Roll out to about 1/2-inch thick on a floured board and shape with biscuit cutter. Bake on lightly greased and floured pan at 350° for about 20 minutes.

Desserts

Kentucky Butter Cake

Juli Duvall—Louisville

3 cups FLOUR
1 tsp. BAKING POWDER
1 tsp. SALT
1/2 tsp. BAKING SODA
1 cup BUTTER, softened

2 cups SUGAR
4 EGGS
1 cup BUTTERMILK
2 tsp. VANILLA

In a mixing bowl, sift together flour, baking powder, salt and baking soda. In another bowl, cream butter then gradually add sugar, creaming well. Add eggs one at a time, beating well after each addition. Stir vanilla into cup of buttermilk. Add sifted ingredients to creamed mixture alternating with buttermilk, beginning and ending with dry ingredients. Grease the bottom of a 10-inch tube pan. Pour in batter and bake at 325° for 60 to 65 minutes, or until cake springs back when touched in the center. Run a spatula around the inside edge of pan to loosen and prick the top of cake with a fork. Pour **Hot Butter Sauce** over top.

Hot Butter Sauce

1 cup SUGAR
1/4 cup WATER

1/2 cup BUTTER
1 Tbsp. VANILLA

Combine sugar, water, and butter in a saucepan. Heat until butter is melted. Do not boil. Add vanilla and mix well.

Aunt Bea's Calico Chippers

"This recipe is a big hit whenever we have a family get-together. I have won Blue and Red Ribbons at the County Fair and the Kentucky State Fair with it. It was one of the nine finalists in the Archway Cookie Contest."

Brenda White—Shelbyville

3/4 cup BUTTER FLAVOR CRISCO®
1 1/4 cups packed LIGHT BROWN SUGAR
2 Tbsp. MILK
1 Tbsp. VANILLA
1 EGG, beaten
1 3/4 cups ALL-PURPOSE FLOUR
1 tsp. SALT
3/4 tsp. BAKING SODA
1/2 cup SEMI-SWEET CHOCOLATE CHIPS
1/2 cup WHITE CHOCOLATE CHIPS
1 cup chopped MACADAMIA NUTS

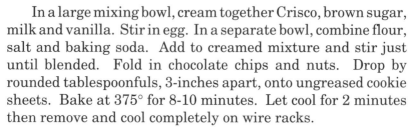

In a large mixing bowl, cream together Crisco, brown sugar, milk and vanilla. Stir in egg. In a separate bowl, combine flour, salt and baking soda. Add to creamed mixture and stir just until blended. Fold in chocolate chips and nuts. Drop by rounded tablespoonfuls, 3-inches apart, onto ungreased cookie sheets. Bake at 375° for 8-10 minutes. Let cool for 2 minutes then remove and cool completely on wire racks.

Yields 3 dozen.

Duncan Hines

Born in Bowling Green in 1880, Duncan Hines' books: "Adventures in Good Eating" (1936) and "Lodging for a Night" (1938), were a must for travelers in the United States. The sign "Recommended by Duncan Hines" became a highly sought after accolade by restaurant and lodging operators everywhere. Hines also published two cookbooks and marketed a highly successful line of processed foods. The Duncan Hines Festival, held mid-June of each year in Bowling Green, honors this famous native son.

Kentucky Derby Pie

Donna Marston—Frankfort

1/4 cup BUTTER, softened
1 cup SUGAR
3 EGGS, beaten
3/4 cup LIGHT CORN SYRUP
1/4 tsp. SALT

1 tsp. VANILLA
1/2 cup CHOCOLATE CHIPS
1/2 cup chopped NUTS
1 (9-inch) unbaked PIE SHELL

In a bowl, cream together butter and sugar; add eggs, corn syrup, salt and vanilla. Fold in chocolate chips and nuts. Pour mixture into pie shell and bake at 350° for 45 minutes.

Triple Crown Winners

To date, only eleven horses have won The Kentucky Derby, The Preakness Stakes and The Belmont Stakes to become Triple Crown winners. They are: Sir Barton (1919), Gallant Fox (1930), Omaha (1935), War Admiral (1937), Whirlaway (1941), Count Fleet (1943), Assault (1946), Citation (1948), Secretariat (1973), Seattle Slew (1977) and Affirmed (1978).

Courier-Journal Cake

"This recipe was named after the oldest leading newspaper in the state of Kentucky."

Norma Barnes—Frankfort

1 box YELLOW or LEMON CAKE MIX
1 pkg. (3.5 oz.) INSTANT
    VANILLA PUDDING
4 EGGS
1 cup COOKING OIL

1 cup SOUR CREAM
1 cup chopped NUTS
1 cup CHOCOLATE CHIPS
1 cup MINIATURE
    MARSHMALLOWS

In a large mixing bowl, combine cake mix, pudding, eggs, oil and sour cream. Beat for 3 minutes. Grease a 10-inch tube pan. Pour 1/2 of the batter into the pan. In a separate bowl, combine nuts and chocolate chips. Sprinkle 1/2 of the nut mixture over the batter then cover with marshmallows. Pour the remaining batter into pan and top with remaining nut mixture. Bake at 350° for 1 hour or until toothpick inserted in center comes out clean. Let cool before removing from pan.

Old-Fashioned 9-Layer Stack Cake

"This cake is best after a couple of days of refrigeration."

Harold Nolan—Loyall

1/2 cup SHORTENING	1 tsp. BAKING POWDER
1 cup SUGAR	1 tsp. BAKING SODA
2 EGGS, beaten	1/4 tsp. SALT
1/2 cup MOLASSES	1/2 cup BUTTERMILK
5 cups FLOUR	

In a large mixing bowl, cream together shortening and sugar. Add eggs and molasses and mix well. In a separate bowl, sift flour, baking powder, baking soda and salt together. Add to creamed mixture, alternating with buttermilk. Mix well until a stiff batter forms. Roll out into 9 thin layers, each the size of a large plate. Bake layers at 350° for 10 minutes. Place cooked layers in freezer so they can be handled more easily when stacking. Place first cake layer on a serving platter and spread with 1/2 cup of *Apple Filling.* Spread to within 1/4-inch from edges. Continue stacking layers and spreading with filling. Top off with the ninth layer of cake. When layering is completed, wrap cake tightly with plastic wrap and let set for 5 hours before refrigerating.

Apple Filling

1 lb. dried APPLES	1/2 tsp. ground CLOVES
1/2 cup packed BROWN SUGAR	1/2 tsp. ALLSPICE
1/2 cup SUGAR	2 tsp. CINNAMON

Wash and cook apples until tender, then mash thoroughly, adding sugars and spices. Set aside to cool.

The Commonwealth of Kentucky

Kentucky is one of four states officially called Common-wealths. The others are Massachusetts, Pennsylvania, and Virginia.

Tutti Frutti

"Fruits from the orchard were used in season to make this topping. Brandy was a special treat, seldom used except for this recipe and for eggnog. This 200-year old recipe is from New Orleans and was used in the early 20th century by my mother-in-law who guarded it carefully. On her copy of this recipe she wrote: 'Best kept under lock and key; very vulnerable to tasters.' You will need a large stone jar with a heavy, tight-fitting lid; metal or plastic will not work. You will also need a long-handled wooden spoon."

Emily N. Thomas—Chenoweth Farm, Shelbyville

1 qt. well-ripened STRAWBERRIES
1 pt. ea. RASPBERRIES, BLACKBERRIES, BOYSENBERRIES,
    BING CHERRIES, diced PEACHES and APRICOTS
1 cup very good BRANDY

Start in strawberry season. Place strawberries in jar; add brandy and stir gently with wooden spoon. As the other fruits ripen, wash and sweeten them, then add to mixture in turn, stirring after each addition. Keep in a cool, dark place, always tightly covered. Topping should be ready for use by Thanksgiving. Once you have opened and used some of the topping, refrigerate the balance. Serve on ice cream or pound cake.

Note: You can combine all of the fruits at the same time if you choose to buy them at a supermarket. Be sure that all are well-ripened.

My Old Kentucky Home State Park
In the 19th century, the occupants of Federal Hill (an impressive antebellum mansion in Bardstown) hosted lavish parties. It is believed that the mansion so charmed Stephen Foster during a visit in 1852 that he was inspired to write "My Old Kentucky Home."

Holiday Jam Cake

"This is the traditional cake for Christmas in our home."

Faye S. Green—Lawrenceburg

1 cup SHORTENING
2 cups SUGAR
5 EGGS, beaten
3 cups sifted FLOUR
1 tsp. CINNAMON
1 tsp. NUTMEG
1 1/2 tsp. ground CLOVES
1 1/2 tsp. ALLSPICE
1/4 tsp. SALT
1 tsp. BAKING SODA
1 cup BUTTERMILK
1 cup seedless RAISINS
1 cup chopped NUTS
2 cups JAM

In a large mixing bowl, cream together shortening and sugar until light and fluffy. Add eggs. In a separate bowl, combine flour, spices and salt and mix well. In a measuring cup, dissolve baking soda in buttermilk. Add buttermilk alternately with flour mixture, to creamed ingredients, beating well after each addition. Lightly dredge fruit and nuts with flour and stir into mixture. Add jam and blend well. Grease and paper-line three 8-inch square cake pans. Bake at 325° for 40 minutes. While still hot, drizzle top with powdered sugar icing, or frost when cool with your favorite frosting.

Orange Balls

"These are fabulous—a good Christmas treat."

Ruby Crooks—Frankfort

1 pkg. (12 oz.) VANILLA WAFERS, crushed
1/2 cup frozen ORANGE JUICE, thawed
3/4 cup sifted POWDERED SUGAR
3/4 cup COCONUT FLAKES
1 1/2 cups chopped PECANS
POWDERED SUGAR

In a large bowl, combine first five ingredients. Use hands to make a smooth mixture and to shape into 1-inch balls. Roll balls in additional powdered sugar to coat. Store in refrigerator in a covered container.

Yields 4 dozen.

Old-Fashioned Boiled Custard

"This recipe has been in my family for five generations. We always make it at Christmas and Easter. It takes time to make, but the end result is worth it!"

Barbara W. McReynolds—Simpsonville

1 gal. MILK　　　　　　　　**2 1/2 cups SUGAR**
10 EGGS　　　　　　　　　　**3 Tbsp. VANILLA**

Pour milk into a large double boiler and heat over boiling water until milk is scalded then allow to cool slightly. (If milk is too hot when beaten eggs are added, mixture will curdle.) Using a wire whisk, beat eggs until light and fluffy. Add eggs to milk and whisk mixture until it coats a spoon. Add sugar and stir until sugar is dissolved. Remove from boiling water and stir in vanilla. Store in glass or plastic containers in refrigerator for up to 2 weeks. Delicious served with cake.

Bourbon Brownies

"These are my favorite brownies. I often make a double batch and freeze half for later use."

Barb Plenge—Shepherdsville

1 lg. box (22 oz.) BROWNIE MIX
1/2 cup chopped PECANS
1/3 cup + 3 Tbsp. BOURBON
1/2 cup + 3 Tbsp. BUTTER, softened
2 cups POWDERED SUGAR
1 cup CHOCOLATE CHIPS

Make brownies according to package directions and add pecans. Spread in a 9 x 13 pan and bake. Remove from oven and cool. Brush 1/3 cup bourbon over top. Cream 1/2 cup butter, powdered sugar and 3 tablespoons bourbon together and spread over brownies. Melt 3 tablespoons butter with chocolate chips and drizzle over top.

Iron Skillet Chocolate Pie

"My mother received this recipe from a co-worker who bragged constantly about her grandmother's pie."

Nancy Greer—Shelbyville

1 1/4 Tbsp. BUTTER
2 1/2 Tbsp. FLOUR
1 cup SUGAR
2 1/2 Tbsp. COCOA POWDER
2 EGGS, separated

1 cup MILK
1 tsp. VANILLA
1 (9-inch) baked PIE SHELL
COOL WHIP®

In a heavy skillet, melt butter. In a small bowl, combine flour, sugar and cocoa powder. Stir into melted butter in skillet. In a medium bowl, beat egg yolks, add milk and beat well. Stirring constantly, add small amounts of egg mixture to ingredients in skillet. Add vanilla and cook slowly until mixture has thickened. Pour batter into pie shell and allow to cool. Top with Cool Whip or meringue.

Aunt Richie's Cobbler ✳

"Whenever we visited my Aunt Richie, who lived in Ashland, she always made this cobbler for our dinner."

Anita Frazier—New Castle

1 cup sifted FLOUR
1 cup SUGAR
2 tsp. BAKING POWDER
3/4 cup MILK
1 tsp. VANILLA

1 can (16 oz.) sliced PEACHES
1/4-1/2 cup BROWN SUGAR
1/4-1/2 cup NUTMEG
1/4 cup BUTTER or
    MARGARINE

In a large mixing bowl, combine flour, sugar and baking powder. Add milk and vanilla and stir well. Grease a 1-quart baking dish with butter and then pour in batter. Distribute undrained peaches over top of batter. Sprinkle with brown sugar and nutmeg and dot top with butter. Bake at 400° for 25 minutes or until tests done.

Double-Flaky Apple Pie

"This apple pie has been a favorite in our home for the past thirty-five years."

Betty Jo Stewart—Bronston

Pie Crust:
2 cups FLOUR, sifted	3/4 cup CRISCO®
1 tsp. SALT	1/4 cup cold WATER

Apple Filling:
6 lg. cooking APPLES, pared, cored and sliced	2 Tbsp. FLOUR
	1 tsp. CINNAMON
3/4 cup SUGAR	1 Tbsp. BUTTER

In a bowl, combine 2 cups of flour with salt and cut in shortening until mixture is coarsely crumbled. Sprinkle with water, 1 tablespoonful at a time, and toss lightly with a fork. When all water has been added, work dough into a firm ball. Divide in half and roll out each to 1/4-inch thickness for top and bottom pie crusts. Layer apples in pastry lined pie plate. In a small bowl, combine sugar, flour and cinnamon, then sprinkle over apples. Dot with butter. Add top crust and pinch edges to seal. Prick top of crust with fork tines to vent. Bake at 400° for 30-40 minutes or until golden brown.

Kentucky Mint Creams

Martie Korfhage—Shepherdsville

2 1/2 cups SUGAR	1 tsp. VANILLA
1/2 cup CREAM	1 tsp. BUTTER
1/4 cup WATER	1/2 tsp. MINT EXTRACT

In a saucepan, mix all ingredients together. Stir well before heating. Do not stir again. Cook to hard ball stage. Pour onto a greased marble slab. When cool enough to handle, pull until candy holds its shape when twisted into a rope. Lay rope on marble to cream then cut into 1/2-inch pieces.

Makes about 4 dozen creams.

Pumpkin Cheese Roll

"This recipe is especially good at Thanksgiving and Christmas. Our former pastor's wife gave a copy of it to all the ladies of our church."

Virginia Spainhoward—Spottsville

3 EGGS
1 cup SUGAR
1 tsp. LEMON JUICE
1/2 tsp. NUTMEG
1/4 tsp. SALT

1 tsp. BAKING SODA
3/4 cup FLOUR
2/3 cup PUMPKIN
1 cup chopped NUTS
1 cup POWDERED SUGAR

In a large mixing bowl, beat eggs on high speed for 1 minute. Gradually add sugar, lemon juice, nutmeg, salt and baking soda. Fold in flour and pumpkin. Spread on a well-greased cookie sheet or in a jelly roll pan. Sprinkle nuts on top. Bake at 375° for 20 minutes. Turn out onto a clean linen dish towel and sprinkle with powdered sugar. Roll up with towel and set aside to cool, 1 1/2-2 hours. When cake is cool, unroll, spread with *Cream Cheese Filling* and re-roll without the towel. Refrigerate or freeze until ready to serve.

Cream Cheese Filling

1 pkg. (8 oz.) CREAM CHEESE, softened
1 tsp. VANILLA
4 tsp. MARGARINE or BUTTER, softened

In a small mixing bowl, combine filling ingredients.

John James Audubon

The famous naturalist, ornithologist and artist, John James Audubon, lived in Henderson for 9 years. Named in his honor, the John James Audubon State Park and the John James Audubon Museum & Nature Center can be found here. At the musuem, see 435 original prints from the 1839 folio edition of his book, "The Birds of America."

Bourbon Balls

"My friend gave me her recipe for these special treats"

Kathy Klusman—Simpsonville

3 1/2 cups POWDERED SUGAR, sifted
2/3 cup GRAHAM CRACKER CRUMBS
1/2 cup finely chopped PECANS
1/4 cup BUTTER, melted
1/3 cup BOURBON
1 lb. SEMISWEET or MILK CHOCOLATE

In a medium mixing bowl, combine first 5 ingredients, cover and chill. Form into small balls and then refrigerate for 10 minutes. In the top of a double-boiler, melt chocolate over hot, not boiling, water. Using a toothpick, dip bourbon balls into chocolate. Place on a baking sheet lined with waxed paper and chill until chocolate hardens. Store in a covered container in a cool area.

Cream Candy

"My mom, Ruth Fairchild, and I used to sell this candy at Christmas time. It's pretty to look at and melts in your mouth."

Alice Rowe—Prestonsburg

3 cups SUGAR
1/8 tsp. SALT
1 cup HOT WATER
1/8 tsp. BAKING SODA

1/2 stick BUTTER
1 cup MILK
1 tsp. PURE VANILLA

In a medium saucepan, combine sugar, salt and water. Using a candy thermometer, cook to soft ball stage (238°). To the center of the mixture (it will be frothy), sprinkle in baking soda and add small squares of butter, one at a time . Add milk by the spoonful, cooking to soft crack stage (260°). Pour candy onto a flat, well-greased porcelain pan. Sprinkle vanilla on candy. When cool, pull into a rope with oiled finger-tips and cut with scissors. Wrap each piece in plastic wrap and store in an airtight container.

Rhubarb Crisp *

"Rhubarb is a harbinger of spring in Kentucky. This dessert is a family favorite."

Virginia R. Robinson—Frankfort

3/4 cup SUGAR
3/4 cup packed BROWN SUGAR
1 stick BUTTER, softened
2 EGGS, beaten
2 cups FLOUR
1 tsp. BAKING SODA

1/2 tsp. SALT
1 cup BUTTERMILK
1 tsp. PURE VANILLA
1 tsp. ORANGE LIQUEUR
2 cups diced RHUBARB

In a large mixing bowl, cream together sugars and butter. Add eggs and mix well. In a separate bowl, combine dry ingredients. Alternately, add buttermilk and dry ingredients to creamed mixture, mixing well after each addition. Stir in vanilla and liqueur, then fold in rhubarb. Pour cake batter into a greased 9 x 13 baking pan and spread *Crispy Topping* over top. Bake at 325° for 40 minutes or until tests done.

Crispy Topping

1/2 cup SUGAR
1/2 cup finely chopped NUTS
1 tsp. grated ORANGE PEEL

1/2 tsp. CINNAMON
1/2 tsp. grated NUTMEG

In a small bowl, mix all ingredients, blending well.

Black Walnut Pie

Tom and Nancy Evans—Kentucky Nut Growers Assn., Henderson

1 cup SUGAR
2 1/2 Tbsp. FLOUR
1/4 tsp. SALT
1 cup LIGHT CORN SYRUP
1/2 cup BUTTER, softened

1 Tbsp. VANILLA
1 cup chopped BLACK
   WALNUTS
1 (9-inch) unbaked PIE
   SHELL

In a mixing bowl, combine sugar, flour, and salt. Blend in corn syrup, butter and vanilla. Mix until smooth. Fold in walnuts and pour into pie shell. Bake at 350° for 45 minutes.

Kentucky Chocolate Chip Pie

"A dear friend gave me this recipe. It is a family favorite at Christmas and also at Kentucky Derby time."

Christine Pollard—Eminence

2 EGGS
1 cup SUGAR
1/2 cup MARGARINE, melted
1 Tbsp.+1 tsp. BOURBON
1/4 cup CORNSTARCH

1 cup finely chopped PECANS
1 pkg. (6 oz.) CHOCOLATE
   CHIPS
1 (9-inch) unbaked PIE SHELL

In a small bowl, beat eggs, gradually adding sugar and mix well. Add margarine and bourbon, then blend in cornstarch. Stir in pecans and chocolate chips. Pour mixture into pie shell. Bake at 350° for 45-50 minutes. Cool. When serving, top pie with *Bourbon Flavored Topping*.

Bourbon Flavored Topping

1 cup COOL WHIP®   1 tsp. BOURBON

In a small bowl, blend Cool Whip and bourbon together well. Refrigerate until ready to serve.

Oldenberg Beer Ice Sorbet

"This sorbet is wonderful. There is a sweetness to beer that, when mixed with the citrus juices, calms down the palate in a delicious way."

Oldenberg Brewing Company—Fort Mitchell

1 cup SUGAR
1/2 cup WATER
2 cups OLDENBERG® BLONDE BEER

Juice of 1/2 LEMON
Juice of 1/2 ORANGE

Bring sugar and water to a boil in a small saucepan. Simmer for 5 minutes. Cool syrup to room temperature, then combine with beer, lemon and orange juices. Place the mixture in an uncovered plastic container and freeze overnight.

Serves 4.

The Original
Kentucky Whiskey Cake

"This cake is very moist and flavorful"

Gardenia Pulliam—Frankfort

1 lb. RED CANDIED
CHERRIES, halved
1/2 lb. GOLDEN or WHITE
RAISINS, halved
or 1/2 lb. DATES, chopped
1 pt. KENTUCKY BOURBON
3/4 lb. BUTTER, softened
1 cup packed BROWN SUGAR
1 lb. SUGAR
6 EGGS, separated
5 cups sifted FLOUR
2 tsp. NUTMEG
1 tsp. BAKING POWDER
1 lb. shelled PECANS

In a bowl, marinate cherries and raisins in bourbon overnight. In another bowl, cream together butter and sugars until light and fluffy, then add egg yolks and beat well. Stir in fruit, bourbon marinade and 4 3/4 cups flour. Add nutmeg and baking powder. Beat egg whites and fold into batter. Lightly flour nuts with the remaining 1/4 cup flour, then stir into batter. Pour batter into a large greased tube pan lined with greased waxed paper. Bake at 275° for 3 hours. When cool, wrap in waxed paper, place in a tightly covered container and refrigerate.

Frankfort
Sometimes called the Bluegrass Capital, this city lies within S-loops of the Kentucky River on a plain surrounded by hills. The north side includes the older residential section, the Old Capitol and the main business district. The New Capitol and the Executive Mansion stand in the southern section. The New Capitol resembles the United States Capitol in design, and is considered to be one of the most beautiful in the country. Frankfort has been the state's political center since 1792, when Louisville and Lexington, both vying for that honor, agreed to compromise. Burley tobacco, corn and bourbon distilling are strong local industries.

Peanut Bars

"My sister gave me this recipe forty-five years ago. These have been a family favorite."

Opal Porter—Taylorsville

2 1/2 cups FLOUR
2 tsp. BAKING POWDER
2 cups SUGAR

4 EGGS, slightly beaten
1 cup boiling WATER

In a large mixing bowl, combine flour, baking powder and sugar. Add eggs and mix well. Stir in boiling water, mixing well. Pour onto a jelly roll pan. Bake at 350° for 20 minutes or until done. Cool before frosting with *Peanut Frosting*.

Peanut Frosting

1 stick BUTTER, softened
4 cups POWDERED SUGAR
4 Tbsp. MILK

1/2 tsp. SALT
2 tsp. VANILLA
2 cups crushed PEANUTS

In a bowl, cream together the butter, powdered sugar, milk and salt. Stir in vanilla and nuts.

Homemade Mincemeat

"This recipe, handed down to my mother from my grandmother, is several generations old."

Mildred Selby—Russell Springs

1 1/2-2 lbs. lean PORK
2 cups MOLASSES
4 cups VINEGAR
4 cups cooked dried APPLES

2 cups SUGAR
1 Tbsp. ALLSPICE
1 box (15 oz.) RAISINS

In a large soup kettle, bring water to a boil then add pork. Cook pork until tender, remove from water, cool and dice. In another kettle, combine remaining mincemeat ingredients; add diced pork. Heat to boiling, stirring constantly to prevent scorching. Cook for 15 minutes, skimming grease from surface. Pour mixture into sterilized jars and seal.

Tom's Maple-Nut Ice Cream

"My great-grandparents, Tom and Emma Reynolds, concocted this recipe in 1917 in Lewisport. Their children, Dick, Kathleen and Magdalene all helped out in the store. People would come from miles around to taste the famous Tom's Ice Cream. Today there is a historical marker on Market Street in Lewisport that commemorates their old store."

Julianne Bibelhauser McClurkin—Shelbyville

1 pkg. (1 oz.) unflavored GELATIN
1 1/2 cups MILK
1 1/4 cups SUGAR
2 lg. cans (12 oz. ea.) EVAPORATED MILK
1 pt. HALF and HALF
1 cup GRAPENUTS® CEREAL
1/2 tsp. MAPLE EXTRACT

In a large saucepan, mix gelatin and milk. Heat to just under boiling or until all of gelatin is dissolved. Stir in sugar, evaporated milk, half and half, Grapenuts and maple extract. Blend well. Make ice cream according to freezer directions.

Makes 1 gallon.

Black Walnut-Oatmeal Cookies

Tom & Nancy Evans, Kentucky Nut Growers Assn.—Henderson

1 cup SHORTENING
1 cup packed BROWN SUGAR
1 cup WHITE SUGAR
2 EGGS, beaten
1 tsp. VANILLA

1 tsp. BAKING SODA
1 1/2 tsp. SALT
1 1/2 cups FLOUR
3 cups QUICK OATS, uncooked
1 cup BLACK WALNUTS

Cream shortening, sugars, eggs and vanilla. Add dry ingredients and mix well. Make dough into a roll and chill in refrigerator for several hours or overnight. Slice into 1/8-inch thick slices. Bake at 350° until light golden brown.

Caramel Dumplings

"My mother only made these dumplings on New Year's Day, along with black-eyed peas, hog jaw bacon, mashed potatoes, macaroni and tomatoes, and cornbread. Eating this meal on New Year's Day is believed to ensure that you will have money all year long, and it works!"

Patricia White—Providence

1 1/2 cups FLOUR	1/2 cup MILK
2 cups SUGAR	Pinch of SALT
2 tsp. BAKING POWDER	1 cup chopped WALNUTS
4 tsp. BUTTER, melted	2 cups HOT WATER

In a large mixing bowl, combine flour, 1/2 cup sugar, baking powder, 2 teaspoons of butter, milk, salt and walnuts. Mix well and set aside. In a large deep iron skillet, caramelize 1/2 cup of sugar. When sugar is light brown, add hot water and remaining sugar. Bring mixture to a boil then add remaining butter. Stir until blended. Carefully drop teaspoonfuls of dumpling batter into hot liquid. Cook at 400° for 5 minutes, stir gently and continue to cook for another 5 minutes or until firm.

Peanut Butter Fudge

"A county fair prize winner! This is ready-to-eat in minutes."
Janet Peercy—Henderson

3 cups SUGAR
1/2 stick BUTTER or MARGARINE
2/3 cup EVAPORATED MILK
1 cup CRUNCHY PEANUT BUTTER
1 tsp. VANILLA
1 cup MINIATURE MARSHMALLOWS
 or 1 cup MARSHMALLOW CREAM

In a medium saucepan, heat sugar, butter and milk, stirring constantly. When mixture comes to a rolling boil, cook for 5 minutes. Remove mixture from heat, add vanilla, peanut butter and marshmallows and beat until thickened. Pour into a buttered dish. Let cool, then cut into squares.

Peach Fritters

"This is my favorite way to use up the abundance of this fresh summer fruit. It is a light dessert, perfect for hot summers."

Rita Flener—Cromwell

2 EGGS	3 cups thinly sliced, fresh
1 cup MILK	PEACHES
2 cups ALL-PURPOSE FLOUR	2 Tbsp. SUGAR
2 1/2 heaping tsp. BAKING POWDER	SHORTENING
1/2 tsp. SALT	

In a large bowl, beat eggs with 1/2 cup of the milk. In a separate bowl, sift flour, baking powder and salt together. Add flour mixture to the egg mixture and then blend in remaining milk. Stir in 2 cups of the peaches. In a small saucepan, place remaining peaches with sugar and enough water to cover. Simmer over low heat until mixture thickens. In a large heavy skillet, melt enough shortening to achieve a depth of 1 1/2 inches. Carefully drop tablespoonfuls of fritter batter into hot shortening and fry, turning once, until both sides are cooked to a golden brown. Remove and drain on paper towels. Place fritters on dessert plates and spoon peach sauce on the top of each. Serve with vanilla ice cream.

Note: Any seasonal fruit may be used in place of peaches.

What's In a Name?

The word Kentucky is generally thought to be from the Indian word "kentake" meaning "great prairie or meadow." Kentucky was originally part of Virginia and was called Fincastle County. In 1792, Kentucky entered the Union as the 15th state. For the first year the capital was located in Lexington, however, a controversy arose between Louisville and Lexington as to where the capital should be located. They reached a compromise and chose Frankfort for the state's center of government.

Apple Cobbler *

"An old-fashioned and delicious favorite."

Odell Stewart—Neon

2 cups SUGAR
2 cups WATER
1/2 cup SHORTENING
1 1/2 cups sifted SELF-RISING
    FLOUR

1/3 cup MILK
4-6 APPLES, peeled and
    thinly sliced
1 tsp. CINNAMON
1 stick BUTTER

Preheat oven to 350°. In a medium saucepan, heat sugar and water; stir until sugar dissolves then set aside. In a large mixing bowl, cut shortening into flour until texture is fine and crumbly. Add milk and stir with a fork until dough does not cling to sides of bowl. Place dough on a lightly floured surface and knead until smooth. Roll dough into a large, 1/4-inch thick, rectangle. Sprinkle cinnamon over apples, then sprinkle apples evenly over dough. Roll up as a jelly roll. Dampen edges of dough with a small amount of water and press or pinch to seal. Slice roll into 16, 1/2-inch thick slices. Melt butter in a 9 x 13 baking dish or sheetcake pan. Place slices in pan and pour sugar syrup carefully around them. Crust will absorb syrup mixture while baking. Bake for 55-60 minutes.

Paintsville's
Kentucky Apple Festival
In early October, 75-100,000 apple lovers gather in Paintsville to enjoy the activities which include a parade, beauty contest, car shows, arts and crafts tents, flea market and concert. A special treat at this festival is apple butter prepared by a local church from a secret recipe that is generations old.

Honeyed Peanut Butter Cookies

"Breathitt County's Honey Festival offers all types of fun in addition to great foods made with honey. There is a bed race, a pageant, the 'Honey Run' and live music."

Clara Gabbard—Breathitt County Honey Festival, Jackson

1 1/2 cups HONEY
1 cup + 3 Tbsp.CHUNKY
  PEANUT BUTTER

4 oz. BUTTER, softened
4 EGGS
4 cups BISCUIT MIX

In a mixing bowl, beat together 1 cup honey, peanut butter and butter. Beat in eggs one at a time. Blend in biscuit mix. With a 1-ounce scoop, portion dough onto parchment-lined sheet pans. Bake at 300° until lightly browned, about 20 minutes. Warm remaining 1/2 cup honey. Brush tops of warm cookies with warm honey. Cool in pans for 5 minutes then remove to racks to cool completely.

Makes 4 dozen.

Strawberry Pizza

O. Dean Borders—Elkton

1 pkg. (20 oz.) refrigerated SUGAR COOKIE DOUGH
2 cups POWDERED SUGAR
1pkg. (8 oz.) CREAM CHEESE, softened
1 tub (8 oz.) WHIPPED TOPPING, thawed
1 qt. fresh STRAWBERRIES, sliced
1 jar (18 oz.) STRAWBERRY GLAZE

Preheat oven to 350°. Roll out cookie dough on cookie sheet or pizza pan to 1/4-1/2-inch thickness. Bake according to package directions or until browned. Let cool. In a bowl, cream together sugar and cream cheese, blending in whipped topping. Spread on cookie dough. Mix strawberries with glaze and spread over top of cream cheese mixture. Refrigerate until ready to serve.

Sheet Brownies with Chocolate Butter Frosting

Tom Schmid—Louisville

2 cups FLOUR
1/4 cup COCOA
2 cups SUGAR
1/2 cup BUTTER
1/2 cup SHORTENING

1 cup strong-brewed COFFEE
2 EGGS, beaten
1/2 cup BUTTERMILK
1 tsp. BAKING SODA
1 tsp. VANILLA

In a large bowl, combine flour, cocoa and sugar. In a heavy saucepan, combine butter, shortening and coffee. Stir and heat to a boil. Pour the butter mixture over the flour mixture. Add remaining ingredients and mix well. Pour into a well-greased jelly roll pan and bake at 400° for 20 minutes, turning pan midway through baking. Pour *Chocolate Butter Frosting* over brownies as soon as they are out of the oven.

Makes 4 dozen.

Chocolate Butter Frosting

1/2 cup BUTTER
2 Tbsp. COCOA
1/4 cup MILK

3 1/2 cups POWDERED SUGAR
1 tsp. VANILLA

In a heavy saucepan, combine butter, cocoa and milk. Heat to boiling, stirring constantly. Reduce heat and stir in sugar and vanilla. Stir until smooth.

The Cumberland Gap

The Cumberland Gap National Historical Park in the southeastern corner of Kentucky, covers more than 20,273 acres and extends into Tennessee and Virginia. Daniel Boone blazed the Wilderness Road through the gap in 1775. Although only a horse path, it is estimated that 200,000 pioneers traveled this path to Kentucky.

Kentucky Food Festival Sampler

FEBRUARY—Annual Buffalo Dinner and Native American Heritage Day. Demonstrations, food and dance. • Kentucky Dam Village State Resort Park, Gilbertsville 270-362-4271

SPRING—Chocolate Festival (one week prior to Easter). Homemade candies, cakes, cookies, pies, fudge contest and Easter Egg hunts. • Old Washington/Maysville 606-759-7423

MAY—Governor's Derby Breakfast (first Saturday in May). A free breakfast with the Governor. Stroll the Capitol grounds for great entertainment and crafts. • Frankfort 800-960-2700

MAY—International Bar-B-Q Festival. Barbeque contest, barbeque in the country as cooking teams compete. Mutton, chickens and burgoo will be cooked, judged and consumed. • Owensboro 800-489-1131

JUNE—Poke Sallet Festival. Three days of fun for the entire family. • Harlan. 606-573-4717

JUNE—Duncan Hines Festival. Honoring its most famous native son. Activities, music, food. • Bowling Green 800-326-7465

JUNE—W.C. Handy Blues and Barbecue Festival. Great jazz and mouth watering barbecue. • Henderson 800-648-3128

JULY—Blackberry Festival Carnival, food and music. • Carlisle 606-289-2384

AUGUST—Stanton Corn Festival • Stanton 606-663-2271

SEPTEMBER

Breathitt County Honey Festival. Crafts, food, games and fun! • Jackson 606-666-7414

Berea Spoonbread Festival. Boone Tavern bread, crafts, food and other fun activities. • Berea 606-986-9760

Floyd County Slone Mountain Squirrel Festival. Famous for its mountain cuisine and crafts. • McDowell 606-886-3565

World Chicken Festival. Crafts, rides, and the world's largest frying pan. • London 800-348-0095

Fulton Banana Festival. Servings of the world's largest banana pudding are free. • Fulton 270-472-9000

Marion County Ham Days. The smell of delicious country ham wafts throughout this festival. • Lebanon 270-692-9594

Monroe County Watermelon Festival. • Tompkinsville 270-487-5504

Trimble County Apple Festival. Festival features arts, crafts, entertainment and a variety of foods. • Bedford 502-255-7196

Paducah's Barbecue on the River and Old Market Days. • Paducah 1-800-PADUCAH

Anderson County Burgoo Festival. This wonderful stew is the centerpiece of this great festival. • Lawrenceburg 502-839-6959

Carter County Sorghum Festival. Crafts, music and a great farm setting complete the charm. • Grayson 606-474-4003

OCTOBER—Kentucky Apple Festival. Crafts, food and entertainment • Paintsville 1-800-542-5790

Index

Index (continued)

Index (continued)

Kentucky Cook Book Contributors

Abraham Lincoln Birthplace National Historic
Site, Hodgenville 22-23, 38, 61, 66
Doris Arnold, Frankfort 47
Kathryn L. Bale, Frankfort 16, 64
Norma Barnes, Frankfort 69
Mae Beshear, Somerset 25, 27
Frances Nell Blanc, Brandenburg 13
O. Dean Borders, Elkton 86
Breathitt County Honey Festival, Jackson 86
Karen J. Burch, Frankfort 46
Louise Butts, Smithfield 37, 47
Heidi Caravan, Mt. Washington 41
Shelby Caravan, Mt. Washington 63
Vera Caudill, Whitesburg 48
Chenoweth Farm, Shelbyville 71
Ann Childs, Shelbyville 20, 33, 34
Clements Catering/Derby Cafe, Louisville 14
Coffee Tree Cabin B&B, Bardstown 17, 19
Joane Cook, Florence 7
Ruby Crooks, Frankfort 72
Marie Cubine, Louisville 13, 26, 58
Juli Duvall, Louisville 44, 67
Jennie Early, Shelbyville 55
Rita Flener, Cromwell 84
Connie Fowler, Stanford 35
Anita Frazier, New Castle 74
Carrie Fulkerson, Sonora 15, 38, 52, 56
Jane Gaines, Henderson 23
Faye S. Green, Lawrenceburg 72
Lynn Green, Waddy 14, 64
Nancy Greer, Shelbyville 74
Edna Guthrie, Eubank 29
Peggy Hagan, Shelbyville 22
Harlan County C of C , Harlan 16
Laura Lee Harpring, Louisville 8, 12
Hodgson Mill, Inc., Hopkinsville 8, 32
The Inn at Woodhaven, Louisville 18, 28
Joan F. Jacobs, Frankfort 59, 61
Mary Ann Jeffries, Henderson 9, 34
Kathy Jo King, Shelbyville 56
Kathy Klusman, Simpsonville 77
Martie Korfhage, Shepherdsville 75
KY Nut Growers Assn., Henderson 63, 78, 82
KY Sweet Sorghum Assn, Clinton 41
Shirley Roberts Louden, Smithfield 52, 55
Donna Marston, Frankfort 60, 69
Lynda Mays, Lexington 11, 19, 31
Julianne McClurkin, Shelbyville 82

Sen. Mitch McConnell, Washington, D.C. 46
Barbara W. McReynolds, Simpsonville 73
Margaret H. Moffett, Shelbyville 30, 36, 54
John Muenks, Shelbyville 50
Lois G. Newton, Shelbyville 39, 54
Harold Nolan, Loyall 70
Old Stone Inn, Simpsonville 13, 53, 60
Oldenberg Brewing Co., Fort Mitchell 21, 79
Osborne's of Cabin Hollow B&B, Somerset 62
John Outlaw, Livermore 58
Tammy Outlaw, Livermore 51
Gov. Paul and Mrs. Judy Patton, Frankfort 12
Ann Peek, Fredonia 51, 57
Janet Peercy, Henderson 83
Barb Plenge, Shepherdsville 73
Nan Plenge, Shepherdsville 27
Christine Pollard, Eminence 79
Opal Porter, Taylorsville 81
Gardenia Pulliam, Frankfort 80
Mary Putman, Henderson 29
Rattlesnake Hill Farm, Bloomfield, 11
Reed Valley Orchard, Paris 10
Mary Reynolds, Eubank 50
Teresa K. Ridgway, Shelbyville 65, 66
Martha N. Robertson, Brandenburg 9, 14, 25
Virginia R. Robinson, Frankfort 78
Alice Rowe, Prestonburg 77
Lauren Russell, Verona 10, 30
Michael Schmid, Louisville 65
Tammy Schmid, Louisville 42, 57
Tom Schmid, Louisville 87
Kelly A. Schweitzer, Shelbyville 49
Mildred Selby, Russell Springs 81
Virginia Spainhoward, Spottsville 76
Betty Jo Stewart, Bronston 75
Odell Stewart, Neon 85
Jean N. Sageser Stodghill, Shelbyville 40
Delana Sue Trent, MayKing 45
Pauline Thomas, Shelbyville 40
Patricia Tindall, Shelbyville 26
Trinity Hills Farm B&B, Paducah 20
Dottie Tyler, Smithfield 48
Brenda White, Shelbyville 68
Patricia White, Providence 83
Cookie E. Whortenbury, Smithfield 33
Susan Wise, Frankfort 62
Sandy Zimmerman, Jamestown 24, 32

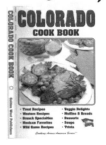

COLORADO COOK BOOK

Bring a taste of Colorado to your dinner table! Sample fishermen's fillets, gold miners' stews, Native American and Southwestern favorites, vegetarian feasts and skiers' hot toddies! Recipes, facts and folklore about Colorado.

5 1/2 x 8 1/2 — 128 pages . . . $6.95

OKLAHOMA COOK BOOK

A roundup of delicious recipes captures the rich cultural and historical charm of Oklahoma. Traditional and contemporary recipes from *Panhandle Pancakes* and *Cowboy Fajitas* to *Chicken Fried Steak* and *Fried Green Tomatoes.*

5 1/2 x 8 1/2 — 96 pages . . . $6.95

ILLINOIS COOK BOOK

Enjoy the flavors of Illinois! Over 100 recipes that celebrate Illinois. *Reuben in the Round, Pork Medallions in Herb Sauce, Autumn's Swiss Supper, Carrot Soufflé, Sky High Honey Biscuits, Rhubarb Cream Pie* to name just a few. Includes fascinating facts and trivia.

5 1/2 x 8 1/2 — 96 pages . . . $6.95

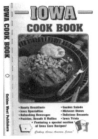

IOWA COOK BOOK

Recipes from across America's heartland. From *Indian Two-Corn Pudding* to *Pork Chops Braised in White Wine* this cookbook presents home-grown favorites and encompasses both ethnic traditions and gourmet specialties. "Iowa Corn Recipes" section highlights this state's most famous export.

5 1/2 x 8 1/2 — 96 pages . . . $6.95

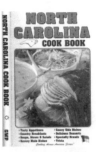

NORTH CAROLINA COOK BOOK

Filled with family favorites as well as recipes that showcase North Carolina's specialty foods. *Sausage Pinwheels, Shipwrecked Crab, Scuppernong Grape Butter, Carolina Blender Slaw, North Carolina Pork BBQ, Rock Fish Muddle, Hushpuppy Fritters, Hummingbird Cake, Peanut Butter Pie* . . . and more!

5 1/2 x 8 1/2 — 96 pages . . . $6.95

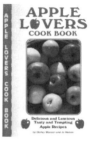

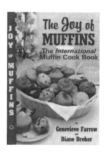

ORDER BLANK

GOLDEN WEST PUBLISHERS

☼ 4113 N. Longview Ave. • Phoenix, AZ 85014

www.goldenwestpublishers.com • **1-800-658-5830** • FAX 602-279-6901

Qty	Title	Price	Amount
	Apple Lovers Cook Book	6.95	
	Bean Lovers Cook Book	6.95	
	Berry Lovers Cook Book	6.95	
	Best Barbecue Recipes	5.95	
	Chili-Lovers' Cook Book	5.95	
	Chip and Dip Lovers Cook Book	5.95	
	Citrus Lovers Cook Book	6.95	
	Colorado Cook Book	6.95	
	Corn Lovers Cook Book	6.95	
	Illinois Cook Book	6.95	
	Iowa Cook Book	6.95	
	Kansas Cook Book	6.95	
	Joy of Muffins	5.95	
	North Carolina Cook Book	6.95	
	Oklahoma Cook Book	6.95	
	Pecan Lovers Cook Book	6.95	
	Pumpkin Lovers Cook Book	6.95	
	Salsa Lovers Cook Book	5.95	
	Tortilla Lovers Cook Book	6.95	
	Veggie Lovers Cook Book	6.95	
Shipping & Handling Add ⇒	U.S. & Canada Other countries	$3.00 $5.00	

☐ My Check or Money Order Enclosed $ _____

☐ MasterCard   ☐ VISA ($20 credit card minimum)

(Payable in U.S. funds)

Acct. No. _____   Exp. Date _____

Signature _____

Name _____   Telephone _____

Address _____

City/State/Zip   **Call for a FREE catalog of all of our titles**   Kentucky CkBk
8/00

This order blank may be photo-copied.